Psychotherapy
with
Adolescent Girls

Doris Lamb

FOREWORD BY DANIEL OFFER

Psychotherapy
with
Adolescent Girls

 Jossey-Bass Publishers

San Francisco • Washington • London • 1978

PSYCHOTHERAPY WITH ADOLESCENT GIRLS
by Doris Lamb

The Jossey-Bass
Social and Behavioral Science Series

Foreword

When I was getting my medical and psychiatric training in the late 1950s and early 1960s, the model of normal and deviant adolescent development was the white male. This was not surprising, since for every clinical or psychological study on adolescent girls done during the past two decades, there were seven studies on adolescent males. This tremendous discrepancy in actual clinical and research data between male and female adolescents led to the following myths: (1) Female adolescents are different only biologically from their male peers; they have similar psychosocial problems; (2) Adolescent girls have not been studied because their problems are not worth studying; (3) Studying adolescent girls might be dangerous to either the patient or therapist, or to both.

In relation to the third myth, male psychotherapists were told that they should not treat female adolescent patients because erotic interplay could develop, which would be harmful to the patient and perhaps impossible to resolve. Many clinics in the United States had a rule that young adolescent girls could not be treated by male therapists. It was thus difficult for girls to obtain treatment—for most therapists were males. It also intensified the feelings among parents, teachers, community leaders, and the girls themselves that perhaps female adolescents were not worth treating.

We still know very little about either the normal or the deviant psychological development of adolescent girls. Much more needs to be done before we will have a meaningful data base from which to compare male and female, young and old, and normal and disturbed adolescents. There are some encouraging indications that we are entering a new era of federally supported research where adolescents in general and female adolescents in particular will receive special attention (see, for example, The Presidential Commission Report on Mental Health, Washington, D.C., 1978). There is also a crop of young, vigorous, and interested female social and behavioral scientists, who have stated that they are specifically interested in studying female development. Much new data will undoubtedly emerge from such research.

Within the context of this momentum, Doris Lamb's book arrives as a timely contribution to a pressing current need. She writes from the perspective of a seasoned clinician who is obviously comfortable in her work with troubled adolescent girls and their despairing families. There is a great deal of clinical wisdom in this book that will help all mental health professionals working with adolescent girls. The many vignettes will surely aid those of us who at times throw up our hands in frustration when trying to help a particularly difficult teenager. I am confident that this volume will also serve interested parents and the public at large because of the wealth of sound clinical advice which the author shares with all of us.

Although there are no simple or quick answers to helping a person in trouble, Doris Lamb has demonstrated how different psychotherapeutic techniques can be of great value to a variety of adolescent girls in the midst of serious psychosocial crises.

June 1978   DANIEL OFFER, M.D.
Chairman, Department of Psychiatry
Michael Reese Hospital and Medical Center
Professor of Psychiatry
University of Chicago

Preface

My work with adolescent girls started more by happenstance than by design. Being a woman probably was a major factor. In any event, over the years I found that many of my referrals were adolescent girls. Referral phone calls from other psychotherapists, school counselors, and probation officers usually started with a comment, made with controlled delight, such as, "I understand you are willing to work with adolescent girls." Very soon, it also became apparent that the significant phrase, "I think she will do better with a female therapist," usually meant that soon an angry, sullen, thirteen-year-old girl would be sitting in front of me, saying nothing, but accompanied by her frantic mother imploring me, "She won't talk to anyone. We don't know what to do!"

In an attempt to increase my skill and self-confidence in dealing with these disturbed adolescent girls, I returned to the literature. I found several significant guideposts that seemed destined to help me in my work. Erikson's (1959) writings on adolescent identity formation and identity diffusion, Aichorn's (1964) essays describing his handling of delinquent boys in Austria, Johnson's (1949) article on children with superego lacunae that they acquired through identification with parents who had similar superego deficits, Gittleson's (1948) essay on character synthesis as a goal of treatment of the disturbed adolescent, Blos' (1967) essay on seeing adolescence as a second separation-individuation, and Josselyn's (1954) writings on the pressures on the ego at adolescence — all were very thought-provoking and helpful in opening my eyes first to look for and then to recognize some of the psychodynamics occurring in my adolescent patients.

Despite the fact that the literature contained these important guideposts, few models could be found for actually doing psychotherapy, and there was little additional theory of practical value. I still felt very alone in my work and very alone in attempting to understand the psychodynamics of my patients' problems and behavior — and much less did I know what to do about them.

In observations of many other psychotherapists who, at first glance seemed to understand the psychodynamics of their patients and the parents of these patients and who seemed to have found a way to deal with the problems, more careful scrutiny revealed that, instead, they were putting people into certain patterns or molds. Actually, they were latching on to only one set of dynamics and one universal solution that they felt could be applied to all adolescent patients and to their parents. One psychotherapist might determine that all parents were too authoritarian and rigid and needed to become more tolerant of their children's acting out. Or, another might see all parents as desperately in need of marriage counseling. Yet another might "discover" that all their disturbed adolescent patients needed to spend more time with other acting-out or disturbed adolescents in an environment where their behavior was more easily tolerated. Certain therapists might refer all patients to adolescent day treatment centers, or to adolescent groups, or to adolescent residential treatment centers. In each situation, one set of dynamics and one treatment approach was being used for all disturbed adolescents.

This book is written to help other therapists who find themselves in a plight similar to my own. It is an attempt to present to readers a practical, yet dynamic theory of the psychotherapy of the adolescent girl. I use case examples freely to illustrate the principles I discuss in the text in the hope that readers will better understand how these dynamic principles can be applied in actual treatment situations. All the case examples are about real people, but I have disguised the patients to the extent that sometimes even I must go back to my original treatment notes to identify them.

I wish to express my deep appreciation to my husband, H. Richard Lamb, also a psychiatrist and author, for his many suggestions and continual emotional support throughout the writing of this book. I also want to thank the many adolescent girls I have worked with during the past fifteen years for all they have taught me.

Los Angeles, California
July 1978

DORIS LAMB

Contents

The Author

Doris Lamb is currently assistant professor of psychiatry at the University of Southern California School of Medicine. She was born and raised in Wisconsin and attended the University of Wisconsin, where she was awarded the B.S. degree in medical sciences and the M.D. degree. She did her psychiatric residency training at Stanford University in Palo Alto, California (1960–1963).

The author has had extensive professional experience dealing with children and adolescents. From 1963 to 1970, she worked part-time at the Childrens' Health Council in Palo Alto, a multidisciplinary diagnostic center for children and adolescents, doing psychiatric evaluations and psychotherapy. Between 1967 and 1976, Lamb also served as consulting psychiatrist to an elementary school special education program, specifically to the learning disabilities program and a special class for emotionally disturbed children; and she was consulting psychiatrist to a halfway house for drug-abusing and emotionally disturbed adolescents, most of whom were on court probation. From 1970 to 1974, she worked part-time as a staff psychiatrist in the mental health unit of the San Mateo County Probation Department, where she conducted court-ordered psychiatric evaluations of adolescents who were detained in the juvenile hall and where she helped set up a peer confrontation group in one of the girls' units. For ten years (1963–1973), Lamb was clinical instructor in the department of psychiatry, Stanford University, supervising the outpatient psychotherapy done by psychiatric residents. In addition, she herself has treated adolescent girls in outpatient psychotherapy for many years.

She and her husband, H. Richard Lamb, have three children, with whom they enjoy the outdoor living of southern California.

Psychotherapy
with
Adolescent Girls

ONE

Essential Concepts

There are shelves of books on adolescence, but in this torrent of words and theories little is relevant to what therapists see in the troubled adolescents that come, or are brought, or even dragged to them for help. Worse yet, therapists can find almost no practical advice on how they can resolve the problems of the disturbed youth whom they wish to help. This book seeks to bridge the chasm between the written word on the one hand and meaningful theory and helpful action on the other.

Most girls pass through adolescence without extraordinary displays of rebellious, negativistic, acting-out behavior. Slowly and progressively they achieve independence from their parents and accept many of their parents' values in the process with surprisingly few of the parent-adolescent tensions one hears so much about. In a longitudinal study of adolescent boys, Offer (1969) found that they were much less rebellious than one might have assumed. Although a similar study has not been done on girls, one can suppose that extreme displays of defiance are similarly

1

not prevalent in adolescent girls. This is an important fact to recognize when treating adolescents in psychotherapy. If a great deal of tension and rebellion is present in the parent-adolescent relationship, psychological problems are probably also present which should be dealt with.

Almost all adolescents, including those who come for psychotherapy, would like to develop more independence from their parents. They would like to do this gradually, and they would like to accept and adopt many of their parents' values in the process. This is an implicit goal for most girls who enter psychotherapy, and the therapist's task is to help these girls come as close to this goal as possible. The adolescent may well complain about her parents; most do. The therapist, however, need not take these complaints at face value, nor should he or she necessarily act on them by helping the girl stand up to her parents, helping her to express her hostility toward them, or helping her to leave home prematurely. Such would be of little benefit to a girl who is not yet ready for premature emancipation. Under the tutelage of a therapist who believes that hostility should be handled by encouraging the adolescent to be more openly hostile, until her parents change or the girl leaves, the girl may find her strained relationships with her parents no longer strained, but severed. She may be able to express her hostility but she has not learned to handle the world any more effectively. Until the adolescent is able to develop her own friends, interests, and occupation, she cannot comfortably leave her family and its social sphere. Premature freedom for the adolescent may only result in loneliness. It is far more beneficial to help the girl slowly grow more independent of her parents.

When working with the adolescent girl, the therapist should develop a treatment plan based on a careful assessment of the psychodynamics of the teenager and her parents. It is important when doing such an assessment to keep in mind that the adolescent is in the process of separating from her parents, that she is becoming a person of her own.

Many factors in the separation-individuation process can interfere with the gradual separation and increasing independence of the girl from her parents. On the one hand, the girl may feel inadequate to deal with the world or she may have so much difficulty finding friends that separation from her parents overwhelms her. As a result, she may begin to develop such symptoms as depression or acting out. On the other hand, her parents may find the prospect of their daughter growing up and separating from them so distressing that they set up roadblocks in her path. They may suggest, explicitly or implicitly, that her leaving will cause their marriage to fail. An impediment of this sort may cause the girl to experience conflict, guilt, and anxiety to such a degree that symptoms of depression or acting-out behavior develop. If the girl has been very close to her father throughout her childhood, the closeness and mutual attraction they feel for each other can pose a threat as the girl becomes physically mature. The anxiety produced by this situation can cause either the daughter or the father to act out. Her father may suddenly become absorbed in a new affair, leaving his daughter feeling abandoned and perplexed. Or, the girl, feeling threatened by the physical attraction to her father, may suddenly become sexually promiscuous, leading to the development of an identity she does not feel comfortable with. Her sexual activity is an attempt to deny her attraction to her father. The separation process becomes more problematic because of the physical attraction.

An assessment of what problems interfere with the adolescent's attempt to separate and to become her own person can help the therapist determine what moves to make in treatment. In Chapters Two and Four, dealing with younger and older adolescents, case examples illustrate some of the problems interfering with the adolescent's attempt to separate from her parents, develop her own identity, and make her own decisions with some degree of certainty and confidence.

Another point to keep in mind is that the adolescent girl's identity is not as fixed as that of an adult. *The adolescent girl can change her identity;* in fact, many do, with or without the aid of psychotherapy. For example, a girl who had become deeply involved in the drug culture, and who did not do well academically, changed on her own. She began to take her studies more seriously, went on to college, and did quite well. Her usage of "street drugs" decreased to socially acceptable proportions over the same period. The change was so drastic that her old friends found her new behavior difficult to understand.

With the aid of psychotherapy, many more adolescent girls can change their identities—girls who would not be able to do so on their own. Becoming involved in psychotherapy can, itself, be a rationalization for change. If the girl has taken a strong stand, insisting to her parents and peers that she will not change, she may feel too embarrassed to go back on her word without the rationalization of "solving her problems in psychotherapy." This principle will be further elaborated in Chapter Two on the younger adolescent girl.

The concept of the ego ideal is helpful in conceptualizing psychotherapy with the adolescent girl. The ego ideal is the idealized self: the person one would like to be, the person one feels one should be. Many adolescents become depressed or act out because they are unable to fulfill the expectations of their ego ideals. Since adolescent girls develop such a strong dependency on their therapists, *therapists can and do function as transient ego ideals* (Teicher, 1973). They are thus able to influence their adolescent patients' standards and goals, helping them to modify their ego ideal so that they will no longer feel that they are failing to achieve previously set standards. Depression over not meeting these standards will be avoided and patients will have new and more realistic standards to live up to.

Often an adolescent girl comes to psychotherapy because she is not able to handle the world around her: she may not be able to find friends; she may be frightened by the loss of security she feels as she becomes less dependent on her parents; she may fear continuing her education or pursuing a vocational program because of the risk of failure; she may not be able to make judgments of other people on her own; and she may not be able to decide whom to trust.

Much of the task of psychotherapy with the adolescent girl is to help her achieve mastery over the situations she faces. She can be helped to learn to find friends. She can be helped to understand how others have felt in similar situations and how they handled similar problems. Of primary importance is helping the teenager to learn to master such problems as how to relate to boys, how to meet people, how to find a friend, how to learn whether or not to trust another person, and how to deal with her parents. Such mastery is an invaluable aid to self-confidence and to the reduction of depression in the adolescent.

Some psychotherapists who work with adolescents believe that the generation gap between the adolescent patient and the therapist can present a handicap to effective psychotherapy. They think that by adopting some of the attire, mannerisms, and jargon of the adolescent they can lessen the gap and improve communication. How strange it must seem to the new or prospective patient to meet such an adult. Any experienced therapist should realize that feelings of empathy, understanding, and interest are not communicated to the patient by attempting to dress and act like her.

There is another reason why therapists should avoid the mannerisms of their adolescent patients. *The teenage girl in psychotherapy needs an adult to relate to.* She needs an adult who is strong enough to tolerate her intense feelings and who can help her learn to handle them. She needs an adult who will try to stop her from getting into difficulties when she cannot stop herself. She needs an adult to teach her what she needs to know about the world.

Therapists working with adolescent girls need to talk more and be much more active than when doing insight-oriented psychotherapy with an adult. If the psychotherapy hour is to proceed at all, the therapist will frequently need to ask questions, suggest topics of conversation, or lead the conversation around to particular problems. The adolescent girl in psychotherapy finds it hard to tolerate the anxiety of silence. This initiative activity on the part of the therapist is more important in the early sessions since, after a few months, the patient will have learned to make better use of the psychotherapy hour. With younger adolescents, the therapist must certainly be more active. The twelve- to fourteen-year-old girl may be shy, or she may find the whole psychotherapy situation frightening and peculiar. Moreover, she probably has not accepted the cultural set of those enlightened adults who feel that it is acceptable and even desirable to walk into the office of a stranger to tell that person their problems. The therapist should inform a new patient of what he or she already knows about her problems; when done in a supportive manner, this will often help her to start talking. It is important to teach the adolescent girl to talk about herself and to help her identify and label her feelings. In addition to not knowing why she feels as she does, she may not know what it is that she is feeling.

Psychotherapists may also find it advisable to occasionally talk about themselves and to allow some of their values to become known to the patient. *The adolescent girl needs a real person to relate to and to identify with.* This is not to say that therapists must reveal everything about themselves to their patients, but, if the therapist is going on a vacation and the adolescent asks where, it is usually appropriate to answer her question. Assuming a modicum of judgment on the therapist's part, there appears to be no harm in talking about his or her car, clothes, or hobbies. As the therapy evolves, it is frequently advisable for therapists to let their patients know how they feel about the use or abuse of "street drugs," sex in a particular relationship, education, or the expectations and limitations of friendships. I am not suggesting lectures on any of these subjects, but an adolescent patient needs to determine, slowly, how the therapist feels about these matters. Personal information about the therapist's children, such as their number, age, or sex, is best not discussed since the adolescent patient can easily see herself in a competitive role, and this can impede therapy.

When doing psychotherapy with the adolescent girl, it is important that the therapist guard against siding with the patient against her parents. Even though the girl may be very convincing in accusing her parents of causing her problems, and even though the therapist may recognize personality characteristics in the parents that could cause difficulties, outright criticism of the parents should be avoided. This does not mean that the therapist cannot allow some feelings of empathy to show toward the girl if she has experienced embarrassment or disappointment because of what her parents have done. Nonetheless, since the adolescent patient may need to live with her parents for a long time, the therapist does not want to take a stance that may widen the gap between them. In addition, therapists must recognize that the adolescent girl, especially the younger adolescent, tends to use denial as a defense. If she receives encouragement in her attitudes toward her parents, she may actually come to believe that her parents are, indeed, her problem—and thus her denial will be reinforced. Now she no longer has problems to work on; her parents are her problem. Many girls who come to psychotherapy, especially older or more mature girls, can learn to adjust to their parents in much the same way as adults can learn to adjust to *their* parents. Adult patients can be helped to see how their parents make them feel guilty, and they can learn to guard against feeling this guilt. An adolescent patient can frequently learn to do the same thing. In Chapter Six on transference and countertransference, the case of Penny illustrates the point that even a younger adolescent can learn to adjust to her mother, despite the fact that her mother did cause her a great deal of difficulty.

Even though the therapist can find evidence of psychopathology in many of the parents who bring their teenage daughters in for psychotherapy, *it is not usually necessary for the parents to undergo psychotherapy themselves.* This philosophy and approach differs from that used in working with younger children, where the child is expected to live with and be at the mercy of the parents' psychopathology for a much longer time. If the adolescent has come, developmentally, to the stage of identity formation and separation from the parents without the need for psychotherapeutic intervention, she is not likely to have been severely traumatized by profound parental psychopathology, and she can learn to adjust to her parents until she is ready to leave them. At any rate, elaborate plans to involve the parents in psychotherapy and to wait for personality changes to occur in them is a bit unrealistic when one remembers that we are talking about a patient who is an adolescent and who thus is growing and developing rapidly; there simply is not time for her to wait for her parents to change. In working out her identity and in separating from her family, the adolescent may need to sidestep whatever interference may be created by the psychopathology of her parents.

Conferences with the parents of the teenage patient may be sufficient to modify the parents' behavior toward the adolescent, particularly when the therapist is willing to give advice to the parents. Advice is most helpful when it grows out of an understanding of the psychodynamics of the adolescent and the parents and when that advice refers to the here and now rather than to the past. Stressing what her parents could or should have done when their daughter was younger helps neither the girl nor her parents. Determining what occurred developmentally is important—the therapist needs to understand past parent-child interactions—but helping the parents understand this is of little benefit. The parents would view an emphasis on developmental dynamics as criticism. They need advice on how to help their daughter in the current phase of her life.

Parents who are genuinely concerned about their teenage daughter are prone to seek advice from her therapist and to try to follow the advice they receive. It is important that the therapist not be seen by the parents as blaming them for the problems of their daughter. The therapist should simply tell the parents what their daughter needs from them and should try to gain their cooperation. The therapist achieves little by trying to show the parents that they have been wrong or insensitive in raising their daughter. A direct approach, telling them what their daughter now needs and asking them to try to provide this, is much more effective. Such an approach also reinforces the positive side of the parents' ambivalence toward their daughter because it is directed to their concerned, parental feelings rather than any revengeful or angry feelings they might have toward their daughter for all the worry or embarrassment she may have caused them. Chapter Seven on advising parents discusses the philosophy and techniques of dealing with the parents of girls seen in psychotherapy.

An adolescent girl in psychotherapy needs to have a feeling of confidentiality about her treatment. But the therapist need not promise to keep everything she says from her parents. Many a psychotherapist has anguished over having made such a promise to an adolescent patient. All too often, when this type of agreement is made, the adolescent patient is tempted to test it out by telling the therapist something that must be revealed if the patient is to be protected from some very self-destructive acting out.

The adolescent girl will usually develop a feeling of trust and confidentiality about her psychotherapy if she is told about every contact between the therapist and her parents. She should be told, not asked, about upcoming conferences between her parents and the therapist because if asked, she might say no. The reason she might say no is not because she cares that a conference is being planned but because she wants to see if she can control the adults in her life. Conferences between therapist and parents are most often necessary with the younger adolescent, and the younger adolescent is not as concerned about such conferences as her older counterpart. At any rate, most adolescents suspect that their therapists and their parents talk about them a great deal anyway.

Sometimes acting out in the adolescent is a counterphobic attempt on her part to try to deal with her fears. The adolescent girl, fearful of the world, fearful of meeting people, fearful of sex, fearful of making decisions on her own, fearful that she cannot handle situations without her parents' help, or fearful that she may never be able to leave home, can act out wildly without any *apparent* fear or concern for danger. Such behavior may result either from an attempt to deal with her fears or to deny them. In situations of this kind, the acting-out behavior will need to be dealt with. If the behavior is a counterphobic move, however, the therapist should help the girl master her fears as soon as possible to prevent further acting out. This situation will be discussed further in Chapter Two.

The acting-out behavior of the younger adolescent is somewhat different in character from that of the older girl. The younger adolescent who acts out is apt to be impulsive and thoughtless in her behavior. She finds herself in the midst of acting out without being aware of how she got started or why. She may not have thought about it much at all; she is impulsive and action oriented. While the older girl may also experience brief episodes of acting out—outbursts that are also impulsive and that seem to clearly be a call for help—the older adolescent is more apt to be thoughtful and purposeful in her behavior. She did not happen to find herself acting out, she chose to do so. Perhaps her friends were doing similar things and she could find no reason to do otherwise. Perhaps she was aware of her parents' embarrassment and either did not care or actually enjoyed it. Perhaps her parents were unclear as to whether or not they condoned her behavior. At any rate, the older adolescent girl is apt to have more control over her behavior and will argue or give reasons as to why she feels it is appropriate to act as she does.

The older adolescent has formed more of her own identity, and this identity may include the self-concept of one who acts out against the social norms. She may see herself as delinquent. *It is important when treating the acting-out, adolescent girl for the psychotherapist to determine something about her identity.* The therapist will want to treat acting out that is impulsive differently from acting out that is part of a girl's delinquent identity. The delinquent girl may continue to act out even though she understands the meaning, origins, and purpose of her behavior. Her identity dictates that she act out.

The psychotherapist who treats the younger adolescent will frequently need to set some limits on her behavior. Such active setting of limits on self-destructive or self-demeaning behavior is sometimes the only way of communicating to the adolescent that the therapist is interested in and concerned about her. Of course, there will be immediate repercussions and protestations about such an active limit-setting process, but the therapist must be prepared to withstand these pressures if he or she wishes to do psychotherapy with adolescent girls, especially with younger girls. It is not easy to set limits on a girl's behavior when she is being seen in outpatient psychotherapy; the therapist will need to be resourceful in finding ways. The parents, for example, can be asked to set limits on their daughter's behavior. If it is overtly antisocial and sufficiently self-destructive to warrant drastic intervention, they can be encouraged to bring her behavior to the attention of the probation department. Or the therapist and parents might consider recommending a short stay in a psychiatric inpatient unit where the adolescent is not allowed many privileges. Sometimes a psychotherapist can limit a girl's acting out just by taking a strong, unambivalent stand against the behavior as inappropriate, dangerous, or both.

If the therapist actively sets limits on the acting-out behavior of a younger adolescent, the transference can be intensified to the degree that the adolescent girl sees the therapist as an extremely powerful, almost omnipotent person. Then, by merely objecting to unacceptable behavior, the therapist can persuade the girl to curtail it. In this type of situation, the girl does not feel that she is curtailing her own behavior; she feels that her therapist is doing this for her. She sees her therapist as a figure powerful enough to accomplish what she, herself, cannot do. Such a transference is best not interpreted until the girl no longer needs this control so desperately. Chapter Six will discuss this omnipotent type of tranference further.

In contrast to the younger girl, the acting out of the older adolescent needs to be dealt with in a more intellectual manner. The older adolescent needs to be convinced that her behavior is disadvantageous to her; she needs to be convinced that she has more to lose than to gain by continuing it. She is also more capable of insight into why she behaves as she does than is the younger adolescent and has more control over her behavior since it is more deliberate and less impulsive. Moves made by her parents to discourage the behavior, such as loss of privileges or clothes, can help persuade the girl that her behavior profits her little. Allowing her to see that her behavior is self-destructive can help to dissuade her. However, if the behavior is to be changed she must be convinced by one means or another to change it; a therapist may need to be innovative to find ways to persuade her to change. When the older adolescent's behavior is definitely antisocial and a part of her identity, peer pressure such as that applied in confrontation groups can be of great benefit in helping her to change. (Peer-confrontation groups will be discussed in Chapter Five.)

Depression when it occurs in the younger adolescent will be rather simplistic in nature. A younger girl who is depressed may be depressed because her mother has told her that she is bad. The depressed girl is usually too closely tied to her mother to question the appraisal. The younger adolescent may not have progressed with her separation-individuation. Without some separateness, she is not in a position to question her mother's judgment. The next chapter gives examples of this type of depression.

The depression of the older adolescent resembles that of the adult. The older girl is apt to be depressed because she fears she will be unable to handle the world. She may be fearful of separating from her parents and become depressed as the time of separation approaches. Her fears of being unable to master her problems can cause her to become immobilized, just as an adult may become depressed and immobilized by the fear of being unable to handle a problem situation.

When treating the adolescent girl, the therapist will have to tolerate a great deal of dependency on the part of the patient. Teenage girls become quite dependent on their therapists. Adolescence is, of course, a time when a girl is separating from and trying to become more independent of her parents, which is not always easy for her to do. Becoming dependent on and confiding in peers is one way she can handle her loss. Her dependency on her parents is thus displaced onto her friends. Yet, the disturbed adolescent may have difficulty finding a friend to become this close to. In our mobile society, where there is less contact with peripheral family members such as grandparents, aunts, and uncles, the adolescent girl may have difficulty finding another adult to become dependent on during the interval between the lessening of her dependency on her parents and the finding of other girls or a boyfriend to confide in. The psychotherapist may be the only adult who will not withdraw his or her support as the girl becomes more independent and self-reliant.

The therapist may also have to tolerate an abrupt ending to this dependency when the adolescent girl no longer needs the therapist so desperately. Finding other teenage girls to become close to, or finding a teacher or counselor at school to get advice from, or being able to confide in a boyfriend is healthy and normal, and the therapist may suddenly not be needed. This rather sudden transition from extreme dependency to no dependency at all can come as a narcissistic blow to the therapist, but if growth and maturation of the adolescent is progressing, all is going as it should. The therapist must gracefully tolerate this change; by doing so, he or she supports the patient's possibly tenuous maturity.

When doing psychotherapy with an adolescent girl, it is best if the therapist does not interpret the transference. The transference of the adolescent in psychotherapy usually serves a need.

To interpret the transference may dissuade the girl from seeing the therapist as someone to be dependent on. If she needs someone to be dependent on, so be it. She may be embarassed and feel belittled if her therapist causes her to see how dependent she really is—not a flattering image for the adolescent who wants to feel independent and strong. If she needs to see the therapist as all powerful (so that she may feel controlled), the transference is best left as is for as long as her need to have it that way remains. Interpreting the transference does not lead to insight as it might with an adult. The adolescent girl will probably alter the transference herself when this becomes appropriate.

To do psychotherapy successfully with the adolescent girl, the psychotherapist must have worked through his or her own adolescence. If the therapist has not yet done so, countertransference problems can arise that will interfere with the psychotherapy. The therapist, in the countertransference, may become overinvolved and overfascinated with the patient's youth. The therapist may rationalize looking and acting like an adolescent as a means to a better relationship with the patient. Such a therapist may, in truth, simply enjoy behaving like an adolescent because he or she overidentifies with the life-style of today's youth. Many psychotherapists were adolescents at a time when sexual freedom and open expression of hostility toward adults in authority was not as socially acceptable as it is today. Under the guise of not wanting to be authoritarian, but because he or she may vicariously enjoy hearing about the acting-out escapades of the patient, a therapist may covertly or overtly encourage even more acting out—even when it is not in the best interest of the patient.

The principles emphasized in this chapter are among those I consider most important in my approach to psychotherapy with adolescent girls. Most adolescents seen in office therapy have problems centering around depression or acting out, and certain patterns and parallels do emerge. The following chapters contain numerous case examples that illustrate recurring problems and situations I have encountered in my work with adolescent girls, and these examples clarify further the therapeutic approach proposed in this book.

TWO

The Younger Adolescent

When a girl in the earlier phase of adolescence comes to a psychotherapist, she is apt to be resistive and defiant. She is likely to question her need for psychotherapy or the value of psychotherapy for anyone. Her impulsive, defiant, self-destructive, and self-demeaning behavior probably brought her to the psychotherapist, and she may well start by refusing to discuss her behavior at all. With that sort of beginning, most therapists feel that they have a tiger by the tail, and they probably do.

Girls in the earlier phase of adolescence are reputedly resistive to psychotherapy, but I believe this resistance can be dealt with and psychotherapy can be successful, *providing* the therapist understands girls in this age group and uses appropriate techniques. If therapy proves to be necessary, the younger girl certainly deserves an opportunity to see if a therapeutic relationship can be established. Advice to parents on how to handle their daughter and some manipulation or change in her environment should also be considered, such as temporarily separating her

15

from her parents' or peers' influence by placing her in a summer camp or school. These interventions can also be helpful for the emotionally disturbed younger girl.

Various writers divide adolescence into either two or three phases with differing ages of onset and ending. I prefer to think of two phases, the earliest starting when the girl is approximately twelve and a half and continuing until she is about fifteen and a half. The later phase of adolescence starts at about age fifteen and a half and continues until age eighteen. In the early period of adolescence, the girl's psychological state is characterized by strong impulses and a relatively weak ego. She is thus likely to act more and think less. Since she thinks about her actions so little, psychotherapy can be a difficult process. It is difficult to help her stop long enough to think about alternative courses of action, to think about why she handled things as she did, or to think about the potential consequences of her actions. She needs to learn to delay acting and to contemplate and evaluate her alternatives.

In addition to impulsiveness, another problem in dealing with the younger adolescent in psychotherapy is an absence of abstract thinking; for example, she is not usually able to think about the pros and cons of a relationship. She likes Carolyn because she likes her. To ask her why she likes Carolyn or what is nice about Carolyn usually produces defensiveness in the younger adolescent patient, who sees implied criticism of her friends in such questions. She doesn't know why she likes someone or why she wants to do something—she just does. The transition to more formal modes of thinking, which, according to Piaget, occurs at about this age, appears not to occur among girls who are disturbed. Many of the younger adolescents who come to psychotherapy do not, as yet, think abstractly, nor do they think in terms of their present behavior having either a positive or negative consequence in their future. Understandably, then, decisions for psychotherapy probably originate outside the girls themselves.

Listening in an interested manner to what the girl has to say—for she loves attention—is a good way to start the therapeutic process. Not only does the adolescent love attention, but prior to coming to psychotherapy she has probably been in many arguments with her parents and she will very likely enjoy having an adult listen to *her* side of the story without shouting at her, criticizing her, or thinking that she is bad. Thus, listening, showing interest, and avoiding being critical constitutes the best approach to starting psychotherapy with a younger adolescent. She wants attention and approval and interest shown to her, and the therapist can offer support in these areas.

The thing *not* to do with the younger adolescent patient is to argue with her "logically" about her situation in order to persuade her to behave more rationally. Possibly only one approach would be worse—to moralize about appropriate behavior. A sermon on propriety or morals could end the psychotherapy immediately. A logical argument or discussion is simply fruitless.

I am not implying that everything the adolescent does should meet with the approval of the therapist. If the therapist believes that the adolescent patient's behavior is self-destructive or self-demeaning or that her actions or behavior are intended as a retaliation against her parents, the therapist must be careful not to agree with the adolescent girl; doing so would only encourage such behavior. But to voice objection to her behavior too readily—say, for example, in the first few sessions, before a relationship has been established—can result in the adolescent not returning for any future sessions.

The adolescent, especially the younger adolescent, will attempt to discover early in therapy whether the therapist sides with her or her parents. She may, for example, complain about her parents not letting her attend a big party and then ask if the therapist agrees with her parents that she should stay at home when everyone else was allowed to go. Frequently these questions are asked in a very provocative way: "Don't you think that a fourteen-year-old girl should be allowed to go to the beach once in a while?" or "Why should Joe have to meet my parents? They never like any of my friends anyway."

The therapist should avoid answering such questions in the beginning. Instead, the girl should be encouraged to provide more information. If pushed, however, the therapist can say that the question is hard to answer, it depends on so many things—sometimes yes and sometimes no. Perhaps her parents had a reason for doing what they did, a reason not yet known to the girl. Another approach is to ask why she thinks her parents took such a stand.

It is not fruitful for a psychotherapist to side with a girl against her parents. In fact, taking either side in the dispute would be counterproductive. The therapist's role is not to put on the black robe to judge who is right and who is wrong but to help the girl adjust to the world. If the therapist mentions some reservations about the girl's acting-out behavior, the girl may view the therapist as being like her parents. Yet, if the therapist is expressing concern for the girl's well-being and wonders if her behavior might be self-destructive or self-demeaning or even dangerous, the therapist will be seen as caring, as being on the side of the girl's well-being rather than on one side or other in the conflict between the girl and her parents. The girl will usually appreciate this concern for her welfare, even though there may be some momentary disappointment because the therapist did not take her side in the battle with her parents.

Usually, by the end of the first hour or two, the girl will ask the therapist for an opinion about her behavior. But if she does not ask, the therapist should be prepared to offer a hint as to how he or she feels about the acting out. It should be *just* a hint and no more. It should come across as a fleeting impression rather than a studied observation or an important pronouncement. At this point in treatment, a strong stand could drive the patient away. Besides, we therapists certainly cannot know all there is to know about a family in one hour or two, so a tentative observation and not a conclusion is more appropriate.

Hearing *any* reservation about her behavior may cause an adolescent to be offended or to disagree. The therapist would do well to let her disagree, saying that the reservation is, after all, just an opinion. "We can disagree. We can talk about it more later and see which opinion is correct." This way of handling the situation suggests to the girl that you, the therapist, respect her as a person and respect her opinion, even though you happen to disagree with it. A disagreement in which the therapist remains tactful may lead her to stop and think about the exchange and possibly even reconsider her own opinion.

A psychotherapist will probably have to confront a patient

about her behavior many times before therapy ends. Tact or perhaps humor or whatever the therapist's style is for producing a gentle and nonthreatening approach is called for. It is possible, and frequently necessary, for the therapist to oppose the adolescent girl's behavior and still communicate to the patient a genuine concern for her welfare.

When an adolescent girl is seen either for an evaluation or for psychotherapy, certain basic assumptions can be made as to what she really wants. She wants to find an identity for herself, that is, to find out what kind of person she is and what she can become; she wants friends, both male and female, with whom she can socialize; she wants to do well in school or at least to avoid failure; and she wants to get along reasonably well with her family. But she also wants to become more independent of her family and to make more and more decisions for herself, thus becoming her own person. She wants to begin to handle the vicissitudes of life and to gain the self-confidence that accompanies achieving mastery both of her impulses and the realities of her world. That is assuming a lot, but that is what most youngsters want for themselves, although they do not always know it at the age of thirteen or fourteen.

Working rapidly with the patient and her family, during the first hour or two, the therapist should attempt to assess the dangers inherent in the patient's acting-out behavior. How self-destructive is the behavior? Is she in real danger? I say "working rapidly," because the therapist will probably be faced with a rather impulsive teenager who may do damage to herself before decisions are made. If the child is actually putting herself in some physical danger, steps may have to be taken to protect her from herself.

Another factor to be assessed when starting psychotherapy with the adolescent girl is her level of progress or achievement in the separation-individuation process which continues throughout adolescence. Has she separated from her parents at all? Does she have friends and activities that do not include her parents?

Sometimes the younger adolescent has made little or no advances on her task of separating from her parents and becoming an individual, that is, her own person with her own identity and with the ability to make decisions for herself with relative confidence. The girl, if she has not separated from her mother to some degree, may not question what her mother says and will adopt her mother's appraisal of situations as her own. This can occur when the younger adolescent is somewhat immature or has spent a great deal of time with her mother. Perhaps, because her mother is an only parent with few outside social contacts or because her marriage is not going well, mother and daughter are very close and have found companionship primarily in each other. It may be the mother's need for the close relationship or the girl's immaturity, or both, that requires the closeness and prevents the normal separation process from occurring.

It is important for a psychotherapist to understand that an adolescent girl who is having difficulty separating from her family will often become depressed and irritable and will displace her irritability onto her mother. The girl may be having difficulties socializing with her peers. She may not be able to find girls with whom she is compatible. She may find that the boys do not like or notice her. Or, she may not yet feel ready to relate to boys and yet feels she should be ready since her girlfriends are. Or, the girl may be reacting to pressures at school or to the frustrations of finding an identity for herself. Sometimes the adolescent is frightened by the many new responsibilities she faces in growing up. Although any combination of these causes for her depression may be present, all that the therapist may see initially is a girl who is very irritable with her mother and complains of many things about her mother that she cannot tolerate.

If the mother remains calm and does not react emotionally to her daughter's attempts to provoke a fight with her but, instead, unemotionally confronts her daughter with the fact that she is in a "bitchy" mood and does not belabor the point, her daughter will not be able to displace her irritability onto her. The girl will more likely be aware of the fact that she is frustrated and irritable because of the problems she faces. But it is very difficult for a mother to react rationally when her daughter is trying to provoke her, especially if her daughter brings her capabilities as a parent into question. If a mother is provoked into arguing with her daughter, the girl releases some of her tensions by arguing.

She may gain some sense of relief but is less aware of her basic problems.

If such bickering goes on long enough between a mother and her daughter, some emotional distance usually develops between them. The daughter has seen her mother angry so often that she likes her less, confides in her less, and somehow solves more of her problems without the aid of her mother, who may tire of the interaction and eventually accept the fact that she has lost her sweet, loving daughter. The daughter's irritability and her displacement of that irritability onto her mother has driven a wedge between them. Because of the distance now established, the daughter is even more motivated to find friends she can confide in and on whom she can depend. The previous dependency on the mother is diffused onto several friends and possibly to another adult she admires. This displacement of her anger resulting from social frustrations onto her mother may compel the adolescent girl to improve her social relationships with her peers. When she is more confortable out in the world, socializing with her peers and with adults outside of her family, the girl can again feel free to relate more closely to her mother. She has effected the separation she needed.

I am not suggesting that these quarrels are the best, or the most common, way to achieve separations, but when the closeness between the mother and the daughter is strong enough to make separation difficult, or if the girl is having difficulties separating for other reasons and needs motivation to continue her quest for independence, they may be the second best way of effecting the process.

Sometimes the adolescent girl is afraid that she will never be able to leave her parents' side. If she is too fearful of the world, or if she is overwhelmed by it because of her own insecurities, she may deny her fears and frantically put herself in all sorts of frightening situations in a counterphobic manner. Instead of feeling her fears, she acts as if she had no fears at all. She convinces herself that she is not afraid to be alone in this world or to run away from home and try to handle the world on her own without money or a place to live. She does not feel fearful of men she meets, and she may have just found a nice man who has befriended her. He has been good to her, and it does not matter that he happens to be a pimp. Somehow the counterphobic girl is able to rationalize in such a manner that she can try things that normally she would be quite frightened of doing. Handling her fears in this way may be effective in accustoming her to the world, but there is so much denial present that she could actually be putting herself into dangerous positions, and she might have to be stopped from such self-destructive behavior. One of the tasks of the therapist is to determine where the pitfalls are, what the problem or problems are that make the adolescent girl's separation-individuation process so traumatic and problematic. The therapist should also try to determine whether or not the girl's method of handling the separation process is likely to be effective and relatively safe.

In the evaluation process, the therapist needs to determine how far apart the parents are when discussing their daughter's behavior. Do they generally agree with each other? Or does one parent, because of marital discord, side with the adolescent daughter rather than with the spouse, even if the spouse's observations are accurate? If one parent sides with the daughter primarily because of negative feelings toward the other parent, the task of psychotherapy is more difficult. It is hard to help the girl see that her behavior is unwise if she has the support of one of her parents.

The therapist should also determine early in his or her contacts with the girl and her parents how psychologically minded the family is. In some families, the degree of sophistication for psychological matters is much greater than in others. Such a level of psychological-mindedness has nothing to do with intelligence; families just differ in this respect. More education might possibly increase the level of psychological-mindedness. Some families have had more exposure to psychotherapy than others. In some subcultures, psychotherapy is valued more than in others and, instead of being stigmatized, one's social status is enhanced by being in psychotherapy. Intellectual interests are even more of a factor in increasing psychological sophistication with the family than is the amount of formal education. Even the type of psychopathology within the family is a factor; people who tend to be depressed, guilt-ridden, and introspective are usually more aware of psychological matters and can more easily handle interpretations of their behavior by the therapist. In any event, tact and caution are always called for.

Early in the evaluation process, the therapist will want to ascertain whether or not any rapport is being established with the patient and whether or not she is beginning to want the therapist's approval. Will she become dependent on the therapist? Such dependency is important, since without it the therapeutic alliance cannot be established and psychotherapy cannot be maintained.

Gittleson (1948, p. 429) states that "Nearly all those who write on the direct psychotherapy of the adolescent stress the importance of a strong, emotionally dependent relationship." He goes on to say that the therapeutic situation needs to be dependable, since the adolescent is so vulnerable, and that this dependability factor is more important than the dependence. This distinction between dependable and dependent is helpful, but both qualities are necessary if psychotherapy with an adolescent girl is to be successful.

Psychotherapy sometimes serves as a face-saving device, allowing a girl to abandon behavior to which she has been previously committed. If the girl adopts such a position, the chances of her continuing in therapy will increase. Prior to therapy, she may have taken so strong a stand against her parents, for so long a period of time, that it is now difficult for her to modify her behavior even if she should wish to do so. She may feel backed into a corner. Sometimes one sees a girl who would like to exchange her identity as a bad girl who does not please her parents for the identity of a girl who has some psychological problems that need to be solved, enabling her to change. This new temporary identity of being a girl with psychological problems is more acceptable to her than feeling that she is doomed to being a bad girl.

Perhaps a girl feels a need to defy her parents and sees no other way to be separate from them except to be very different. If a girl feels that there are many things about her parents that she likes, and if she has been very close to them, she may have difficulty finding her own identity. If she truly admires one of her parents in a fashion akin to hero worship and lacks the security and strength to develop her own individuality, she may then act out against her favored parent and behave in almost an opposite manner in order to find an identity of her own. Being different from her parents for a while does allow a girl to feel that she is developing her own identity and not just remaining one of her parents' children. A younger adolescent girl does not think these things out, of course. She may have some such concern ever so briefly, but usually these conflicts are unconscious.

After a while, she may feel that she has effected the separateness she needs but fears she has gone so far in being the opposite of her parents that they no longer approve of her. She may want to again be the person her parents wished her to be. But doing so is difficult for many adolescents. It might mean taking back all she has said she stood for. If she starts psychotherapy, admits that she has some problems, and lets herself be "cured" or overcomes her problems, she can follow her parents' wishes and be a "good" girl again without feeling guilty for having caused her parents so much anguish. The adolescent girl in such a process exchanges the identity of being a bad girl, who does not please her parents, for the temporary identity of being a girl with some psychological problems and in need of psychotherapy. She then again changes her identity to being a good girl who pleases her parents.

The adolescent patient, especially the younger one, does not have the fixed identity that the adult psychotherapy patient is likely to have. The adolescent girl can and does change her identity. The therapist can frequently help her change to an identity that will be less self-destructive and more profitable and comfortable for her in the years to come.

When an adolescent girl starts in psychotherapy, her parents, now seeing their daughter as having psychological problems, may be less angry with her and more willing to try to help her by doing the kind of parenting that the therapist feels is advisable. Parents often feel relieved that psychotherapy has started and that they are no longer solely responsible for their daughter's well-being. Such a softening in the parents' attitude is also a factor increasing the likelihood that the therapy will continue and will be successful.

In the case of Christy, we see an example of a girl in the

earlier phase of adolescence who could not handle her impulses and who appeared to want help with this problem. She became quite dependent on the therapist, and this dependency seemed to help her gain control over her impulses. We can also see in Christy's treatment the value of environmental manipulation.

Christy was a fourteen-and-a-half-year-old girl whose parents brought her in for psychotherapy and asked for advice on how to deal with her. She was deeply involved with a twenty-year-old man of whom her parents disapproved most strenuously. The young man was unemployed but made some money rebuilding and selling cars. Having dropped out of high school, he lived alone and appeared to have no plans for the future. He was now on probation with the adult probation department and had also been on probation as an adolescent. Christy had been going with him for almost three years and saw him daily, frequently skipping school to do so. Her grades were terrible and it appeared she would not finish high school either.

In a family conference held early in the evaluation, Christy was adamant in her accusations against her parents, reminding them of their many faults; the parents agreed with what she said. Her mother was constantly trying to save money by buying things from Goodwill and had a cluttered, unkempt house full of her bargains, an embarrassment to her daughter. Whenever possible, her father would invest money in an obviously failing business venture. He also liked to shop for groceries and would buy more food than the family could possibly eat. Her mother shopped for bargains to save money; her father spent more money than she felt necessary. The family was in debt to a loan company and as soon as the debt decreased, they borrowed more. The father, who complained that the marriage was bad, refused to get involved in what he regarded as his wife's pettiness of saving pennies. He feared becoming depressed again if he stopped his free-spending ways. He had just recently been through a period of depression that had been helped by psychotherapy.

In the evaluation interviews with Christy alone, the girl complained of her appearance, saying she was fat. When it was pointed out that her weight was certainly not an obvious problem, she only said that she had been thinner and wished to be so again.

She complained of her inability to resist eating and her inability to resist 'seeing the young man her parents disapproved of. She said she frequently climbed out a window at night to see Jeff and thus was too tired to go to school in the morning. She knew her parents were right about his not being a good influence on her, but he had been controlling her for the past two years. Jeff had been like a parent or a hero to her. He wanted her to be thin, so she stayed thin to please him. By insisting that she see no other boys, he seemed to help her control her urge to run wild. She felt that he had practically raised her. Although she did not say so, it appeared that she desired the external controls as well as the attention he gave her. She felt that there was no way she could stop seeing him; she described it as an addiction. Yet, she knew she could not like herself if she did *not* stop seeing him.

Although Christy was fond of her three older sisters, she had always been critical of the one who had no education or training beyond high school and who settled for marrying a continually unemployed man who lived on welfare. She was afraid she was choosing a similar fate for herself. Christy described her young man as dreading any competition. He did not want her to go to school or to make anything of herself because he feared he would not be able to control her any longer and would lose her. If she wished to accomplish more with her life than her sister had, she felt she must stop seeing Jeff.

Christy and the therapist decided that the best thing to do would be for her to go away for a while, live apart from Jeff, and learn to be more self-reliant. Then she might be able to decide if she wanted to see him or not; she might then have a choice.

Christy knew how to make her parents feel guilty by pointing out their poor parenting. Her parents were aware they neglected Christy because they had been preoccupied with themselves. She purposely made them feel guilty in a family therapy session to persuade them to pay for her support so that she could visit a family in another city for six months.

Christy did go away and returned six months later, now wanting to be home and feeling that she could handle things better. It was still difficult for her to handle her impulses, but she did manage to attend school and eventually graduated. On very rare occasions she would see her old boyfriend, but she never became sexually involved with him again. Eventually, she found another young man who was somewhat more achieving and more acceptable to her parents.

The case of Christy illustrates the impulsiveness of the younger adolescent girl. Christy had run to her young man over and over again for three years. Only now was she thinking about the relationship and questioning its wisdom in terms of her future. But by now, she was addicted to him. Although she had acted without thinking at the outset of the relationship, she was now able to reflect about her situation.

The clarity with which Christy could explain her problems was noteworthy. She said that she had to stop seeing Jeff in order to think well of herself and that she would be depressed if she did not stop seeing him. Christy came from a psychologically sophisticated family. Her father was in the habit of discussing his children's emotional reactions with them. Their relationships with other people were also frequently discussed. Her father had been in psychotherapy himself and had found it a good experience. He had not felt stigmatized by the treatment and could talk of it with his coworkers and even gain social prestige for being in psychotherapy.

Christy's dependency on the therapist, which developed readily, was important in her treatment. She needed someone to be dependent on so that she could lessen her dependency on her boyfriend. Yet, it would be difficult for her to go back to being so dependent on one of her parents. At her age, her developmental task was to separate from them, not to return to dependence. Christy needed another adult to depend on and the therapist served as this person.

The manipulation of the environment, which was created by sending Christy away to live with a family for six months, was also very helpful in her treatment. It gave her a moratorium from seeing the boyfriend and allowed her time to think and to see herself in perspective. She also used this time to socialize with other young people. She had one boyfriend for three years; her social interactions were only with Jeff as "his girl."

The case of Debbie is an example of an adolescent girl who

was angry with her mother and who accused her of behaving poorly at a time when she was attempting to separate from her. Debbie's accusations of her mother were so convincing that she persuaded herself that she must leave home. Even though Debbie's therapist did not side with her against her mother, the therapy went well.

Debbie, thirteen years old, was referred for psychotherapy by her probation officer. Debbie had run away from home and remained away for about two weeks, spending the time with an older teenage boy. When she was found, Debbie was taken to a juvenile hall detention center for juvenile offenders. She adamantly refused to return home to her mother and stepfather and was temporarily placed in the home of a couple with three children who lived in her neighborhood.

Debbie's probation officer could find no compelling reason why she should not return home, and he felt that psychotherapy might be in order. Debbie was eager to enter therapy and stated that she did not have a *specific* problem but that she was always unhappy and knew that she must have some psychological problem. It was amazing to hear a thirteen-year-old talk with such sophistication. Not until some time later did it become clear that she was a lonely girl who wanted attention and knew just what to say to please people. She was trying to please her therapist.

Debbie said that she had run away because she could no longer tolerate living with her mother. She complained that her mother drank heavily every day and that she became irrational and angry as a result. Debbie said she could no longer tolerate her mother's drinking. She also complained that her mother encouraged her to miss school. Her mother worked and found it convenient for Debbie to stay home with the twins, children from the mother's second marriage. Debbie talked of the fun she had when not in school. For weeks at a time she would stay at home and be kept company by other youngsters, usually boys older than herself. The house apparently was a place for them to hang out. Debbie, however, did not become sexually active until later, when she ran away.

Debbie had tried a year earlier to live with her father and his second wife. She found life in the suburbs boring. She also said that she could not stay there because she did not know any of the children in the area. She described behaving disagreeably toward her father's wife. She complained to her father about his wife every day, despite the woman's efforts to take her places and buy things for her. Debbie's complaints to her father about his wife were vague. For example, Debbie said, "Nora only takes me places she wants to shop." Debbie recognized that she was complaining with no real justification and admitted that she enjoyed causing difficulties between her father and his wife. However, she did not know why she wanted to be so difficult.

In the course of therapy, Debbie became quite dependent on the therapist. She was seen in therapy for a series of sessions three times, each series interrupted when she returned home to live with her mother. When away from home, she came to see the therapist regularly and seemed to enjoy the attention, listening to any suggestions the therapist made and trying to understand her behavior.

It became apparent that Debbie frequently set up situations in which two people fought over her. Such was the case with her parents. Before going to live with her father, she wrote and called him many times to complain about her mother's behavior. He became very distressed and sent her a plane ticket so she could come to stay with him. Yet, soon after Debbie arrived at her father's home, she contacted her mother, who pleaded with Debbie to return home to her since she missed her so much. Debbie resisted returning to her mother initially but she told her mother all about the injustices she suffered at the hands of her father's wife. It was easy for Debbie to convince her mother that Nora was a terrible person but it took about three weeks for her to convince herself of this. Her mother continued to beg Debbie to return. The strong, mutual need for each other prevailed and Debbie left in the middle of the night; her mother also sent her a ticket. Debbie's stay with her father lasted only three weeks.

Debbie stayed in her first foster home for three months. Occasionally she went home to see her mother, who lived down the block. Her mother, at such times, tried to persuade Debbie to come home to live. Debbie refused and told her foster mother and her therapist that her mother was begging her to return. Her foster mother became furious with Debbie's mother for bothering the girl. Debbie eventually did go home and remained there until her next runaway.

The pattern repeated itself at Debbie's second foster home. Eventually she came to see that she played her mother off against her various foster mothers, getting them to fight over her just as she had gotten her parents to fight over her. Debbie also came to see that she did the same thing with the boys in her life. She always had two boyfriends, both of whom competed for her attentions. Although she recognized that she did this, she wasn't sure why. She knew that she liked the attention and the security that came when people fought over her, but both she and her therapist knew that there must be a further explanation for her actions.

Eventually Debbie found herself in a foster home that she liked. The foster mother did not try to be a parent to Debbie but let her come and go as she wished, just as the other foster daughters in the home did. She insisted, however, that all the girls go to school regularly and that they do their homework. During this period, Debbie once again saw her therapist. She was attending school and working in a hamburger stand. She was able to get the job because she lied about her age and because the assistant manager, a young man, fell in love with her. Although she did not plan it that way, she became very fond of him also, and they wanted to marry. They could not do so, however, because Debbie was still fifteen and under the supervision of the probation department.

Debbie, at this time, was able to talk about her earlier fears of never being able to leave home. Although she had complaints about her mother, she recognized that her mother did give her almost everything she wanted. Her mother was always there to protect her, help her, and even lie for her. Later, it came out that it was as much Debbie's idea to miss all those days of school as it was her mother's. If Debbie wanted an excuse from school, her mother lied for her. Although her mother's drinking was not to Debbie's liking, that problem had always been there and it did not change. Debbie certainly did not like her mother's drinking, but she had grown accustomed to it through the years. Children learn to live with many idiosyncracies of their parents, and Debbie had learned to live with her mother's drinking. She did not complain about her mother until she became an adolescent. Because of the mutual closeness and mutual dependency between Debbie and her mother, separation from her mother at adolescence was a problem for the girl. The bond between them was so strong that Debbie felt a serious loss when she tried to do things on her own. Since she had missed so much school, she felt all the more incapable of leaving her mother's side and facing the world. Not only had she missed out on a great deal of education, but she had also missed the socializing and problem-solving experiences that children have when they adapt to school and to the teachers and their peers. Debbie had not faced the problems or learned the mastery of the problems that most school-age children have. This lack of skills, together with the dependency on her mother, made separating from her mother frightening. Debbie seized upon her mother's drinking—she complained about it so often and to so many different people that she convinced many of them that she must leave her mother. And, by talking about her mother's drinking so much, she also convinced herself that this was, indeed, an intolerable situation and that she must leave. Debbie's sojourns to her father's home and to various foster homes were attempts to get free of her mother's domination and protection and to try to live in the world without her mother's help. Debbie eventually learned to do this. Living away from home and away from her mother and learning to cope with different living situations (with advice from her therapist) helped her gain a sense of mastery.

When she terminated her therapy, Debbie felt she no longer needed help. She expressed appreciation for the therapist's support and advice but said she wanted to try to manage on her own. She could have continued to receive treatment under Medicaid, but she wanted to try to make her way in the world without her therapist. This was something Debbie needed to learn to do. Debbie had learned to manage without her mother; now she needed to learn to manage without her therapist.

In Debbie's case we see an adolescent girl who was fearful of leaving her mother's side but who repeatedly ran away nonetheless, seemingly without fear. The "I'm afraid to leave" thoughts were changed to "I must run away" thoughts in a typically counterphobic manner. Debbie's case also illustrates the younger adolescent who displaces her anger and frustration over her fears and social problems by blaming her mother. True, her mother did drink, and Debbie found agreement from others that this behavior was objectionable. Many adolescents who displace their anger and frustrations onto their mothers have no such convenient target. Debbie's blaming her mother was not a conscious manipulative move but an unconscious denial of her fears. She really convinced herself that she must leave because of her mother's drinking. If she had faced the fact that she was not reacting to her mother's drinking, Debbie would have been forced to face her own fears and might have been overwhelmed by their intensity.

Even though Debbie was able to paint a terrible picture of her mother for her therapist, the therapist never did agree with Debbie that the mother was wholly to blame. Debbie never expressed any disappointment about this. In fact, Debbie came to dislike two of her foster mothers because she had been able to convince them that her mother was the cause of all her problems. She even expressed some bitterness that they dared to hate her mother when her mother had never caused them any harm. It can be dangerous for a therapist to side with the adolescent patient against her parents.

In the case of Anne, we see another instance of a girl in the early phase of adolescence who could not control her impulses to run to boys and became depressed because of her lack of control. Her own ego ideal, or standards for herself, could not condone her promiscuity. Her behavior may have been the result of the strength of her sexual drives, but it probably was a retaliation directed toward her father. In Anne's treatment, we again see the helpfulness of environmental manipulation and the great dependency on the therapist so characteristic in psychotherapy with the adolescent girl.

Anne, fourteen years old, was brought for an evaluation by her mother, who was extremely worried that her daughter's reputation was becoming ruined because Anne could not stay away from boys. The family, socially polished and achievement oriented, lived in an affluent area. The father was a vice-president of a large corporation and the mother did all the "right" social things comfortably and raised their two children with care and interest.

Anne, a strikingly attractive girl, was well mannered, poised, and well spoken, and showed the evidence of considerable efforts on her mother's part to dress and train her. Despite all of her mother's efforts, Anne had quite recently become involved with boys and indiscriminately slept with many of them even without really dating or having a boyfriend. Her mother would drive her and a friend to a Saturday movie and pick her up later, only to find out that Anne had spent the time downtown with boys and had not seen the movie at all.

In the evaluation hours, Anne talked little when alone except to offer some objections to her mother's overprotection. She appeared to be unhappy with herself, but certainly did not say so; she appeared very sad and embarrassed. Anne's mother reported that the father could not come in for a meeting with the therapist because he was extremely busy at work at this time. He was, in fact, so busy with new projects at work that he had taken an apartment close to work so that he would not have to commute—a fifteen minute commute! Eventually the mother admitted that her husband was having an affair; she did not want to admit it publicly because then she might have to do something about it, such as end her marriage. She hoped this affair was just a phase for her husband. Although she was not able to share this information with the therapist until six months after therapy started, the situation was quite obvious from the outset.

Anne and her father had been very close and had always enjoyed each other's company. Anne had always seemed infatuated with her father, but when she was a little girl no one had thought it unusual. Now that she was an extremely attractive adolescent girl, this closeness between them may have been a problem for her father. He was having an affair—unusual behavior for him. Perhaps his attraction and closeness to his daughter frightened him when the girl developed into a lovely young woman. I have seen this situation many times in my work: The girl and her father are very close, and, when the daughter matures to an attractive adolescent, her father suddenly and unexpectedly has an affair with a new love.

Anne reacted very strongly when she learned of her father's affair, as do so many adolescent girls who have earlier enjoyed a special closeness and mutual attraction with their fathers. The girls seem to be bothered more than their mothers. Some girls in this type of situation become depressed and full of self-pity. Some react with extreme anger and righteous indignation, saying, in effect, "How dare Daddy do that to *me*!" Some girls react as Anne did. Anne became depressed and then acted out in retaliation by becoming sexually involved with boys. She was depressed enough to behave in this self-deprecating manner. In addition, she became even more depressed because her behavior lowered her self-esteem. She could not respect herself because she let her anger and depression cause her to lose her self-control. A nearby, private girl's boarding school was recommended for Anne, along with office psychotherapy; these recommendations were followed.

At first, Anne did not talk much to the therapist and a therapeutic relationship did not appear to be developing. But when Anne began boarding school, a change occurred. Her first office visit from school began with her usual pleasantries; she was trained to speak to adults politely and with poise. But when asked if she were homesick, Anne began to sob uncontrollably. She quickly became very dependent on the therapist and began to look forward to the visits and talked of such things as being homesick, of being socially uncomfortable, and wondering how the other girls could find close girlfriends so easily. She was puzzled about the little hostilities of cliques at school; she needed to learn about the world and to decide such things as which type of girls she would like to associate with. Eventually she even started talking about boys.

When her self-demeaning behavior of sleeping around was stopped, Anne's depression improved and the task of helping her understand the ways of the world and other people proceeded. Anne had played the role of "daddy's little girl" for too long and had always accepted the opinions and attitudes of her parents as her own. As a result, she had much to learn about dealing with the frustrations and demands of the world. As she learned about such matters from her therapy, Anne's self-esteem increased and her depression lightened. She liked herself more when she felt comfortable in the young adult role and when she was able to control her impulses.

When she started talking about boys, dating, and sex, Anne approached it as a previously taboo subject. After all, boys were the apparent reason she was sent to psychotherapy and boarding school. She wanted to know if the therapist approved of her even thinking about boys, and later she wanted to learn from the therapist how to talk to boys and how to date. She knew how to have sex but did not know how to establish a relationship.

Early in the therapy and not long after Anne became a boarding student, her father returned home and the marriage appeared to be going well. After a year, Anne went home to live, although she continued at the same school as a day student and remained in therapy for the rest of the school year. For several years following termination of the psychotherapy, Anne or her mother would occasionally call or send a note indicating that all was going well and that they appreciated the timely help.

Anne's therapy may be considered a success. The girl was no longer depressed, she socialized, had friends, and did well in school. Yet the basic closeness to her father—the possible impetus for his affair—was never a subject for therapy or parent conferences. A basic knowledge of the psychological processes occurring in the adolescent girl and in her family are essential if the therapist is to make the best therapeutic moves and give the best possible advice and counsel, but all that the therapist sees or suspects does not need to be discussed with or interpreted to the patient. Many things are better left unsaid. A threatening interpretation to this psychologically unsophisticated family would have been too much for them to handle. It took the patient and her mother many months to even acknowledge that an affair was occurring, and then they said it so tearfully that it could not be discussed. The father never did find time to see the therapist.

In her classic article on psychotherapy with the younger adolescent girl, Fraiberg (1955) states that she prefers to talk with the patient about seemingly unimportant things, such as clothes and everyday happenings in school. She prefers to spend most of the therapy time with the younger adolescent in such apparently trivial discussions, making only occasional interpretations and then not pressing them. Fraiberg feels that these seemingly unimportant topics are the adolescent's realities.

I certainly agree that the seemingly unimportant therapy topics that the younger adolescent usually brings up are actually important; they are indeed the adolescent's realities. What to wear to make the right impression is a big thing. How to understand other adolescents, especially adolescent boys, and adults is very important for the young adolescent girl. But I would carry Fraiberg's notion a bit further and suggest that interpretations be made rarely, rather than occasionally, unless one is working with a rather psychologically sophisticated family with previous psychotherapy experience.

In all three cases mentioned so far in this chapter, there were occasional contacts between the therapist and the parents of the patient early in the therapy. (Although Debbie's mother never saw the therapist, she did call.) These contacts between therapist and parent appear to pose little threat to the relationship between the therapist and the younger adolescent. It is certainly advisable to tell the adolescent girl ahead of time, if possible, that a conference with her parents is scheduled. When this is not possible, the girl should be told afterward. The general content and tone of the discussions can be shared with the girl but in a matter-of-fact way that does not put undue emphasis on the importance of the parent-therapist contact.

In the case of Terry, the ability of a disturbed younger adolescent to change her identity is described. Terry was a fourteen-and-a-half-year-old girl who was admitted to the juvenile hall for having run away from home and for having stolen some things from a drug store while "on the run." Terry was away from home for only two days; she was caught the very first time she tried to steal. She lacked the sophistication of many of the more delinquent girls who are able to manage on the streets after running away from home.

The supervisors in the juvenile hall asked the unit psychiatrist to see Terry shortly after she was admitted. She was adjusting so poorly and seemed so different from the usual girl detained that the supervisors were concerned about her. They also found her quite irritating. She wanted a great deal of attention; she whined a lot and expected the staff to take care of her as if she were a much younger girl. She seemed unaware of what was going on about her.

The other girls in the institution quickly learned that Terry was different from them; they were hostile and mocked her. As a result, the staff was concerned that she would not be able to relate to the other girls and might even be harmed by them.

In her interview with the juvenile hall psychiatrist, which occurred on her second day in the hall, Terry reported a history of several psychiatric hospitalizations plus outpatient psychotherapy over the course of the last two years. She said that she had difficulty relating to other girls and had never had a boyfriend. She lived with her parents and two siblings, an older girl and a younger brother. Her father, who was employed by the Veterans Administration, had insurance to pay for her therapy and hospitalizations. Her mother was not employed outside the home.

Terry had never done well in school. She was always slow to socialize and had wet her bed and sucked her thumb beyond the expected age. She was somewhat obese and could identify no area of her life in which she had been successful. Her siblings had fared better; they had friends and were more successful in school. None of the children, however, excelled academically or took school very seriously. Terry was always, at least as far back as she could remember, teased by neighborhood children and was the scapegoat for other girls in her class. She felt very much a failure. She said she was enjoying the attention that she was receiving for running away from home, even though she had been scared all the time she was away, and that she enjoyed being considered delinquent. She came from a neighborhood where many of the girls had been in that juvenile hall, and she seemed to feel that her being sent there was somewhat of an accomplishment.

Her outside therapist was contacted the day following Terry's interview with the psychiatrist to determine if arrangements could be made to rehospitalize Terry. He stated that although he had tried, there had been little progress with Terry's treatment. He hoped that the experience she was having in the juvenile hall would benefit her. He did not believe that she was psychotic, but, rather, that she was unable to adjust to the world and did not know how to relate to her peers. He considered her to be very inadequate.

The psychiatrist could not reach Terry's parents until the fourth day the girl was in custody. The parents were somewhat relieved that their daughter had landed in juvenile hall. Perhaps now she could learn something. They had been to the parents' group at the juvenile hall the night before and felt that there was adequate therapy for their daughter in that institution; they did not wish to have her transferred to a psychiatric hospital; they had tried that before. It appeared that no one, neither the girl, her parents, nor her therapist, wanted her to leave juvenile hall at that time. Perhaps all who had tried to help her were feeling anger and frustration. At any rate, it appeared that Terry was to remain at the institution for a while, at least until the court determined her future.

In interviews with the juvenile hall psychiatrist, Terry complained about not being able to get along with either the girls or the staff. She said that everyone seemed angry with her and she did not know why. She had experienced the same thing outside the juvenile hall — at school and in the neighborhood — and appeared to have no idea of the sort of things she did that irritated people. The therapist asked her to talk about the most recent time one of the staff members was angry with her. This had happened, Terry said, just a minute ago. She had wanted to wash her hair and asked a staff member to give her some shampoo. The staff member had then become angry with her for no apparent reason. Terry was asked by the psychiatrist if she knew when shower time was. She said she did know, that it was in the evenings after dinner. "Then why did you ask for the shampoo at 11:00 a.m.?" asked the psychiatrist. "Because my hair was dirty, and I was too tired to wash it last night." "You were aware of the fact that it wasn't the right time to wash your hair and yet you asked for the shampoo?" "Yes." "Why?" "I don't know," she said, "but my therapist on the outside said that I did things to get attention."

Terry did a great many things to get attention, but it also

appeared that she was unable to relate feedback to her actions. For example, she succeeded in getting the other girls angry with her by telling a staff member whenever one of the girls would break a rule. Yet she knew that no one in any juvenile hall likes a "snitch." When confronted, she would say that it just slipped out and she didn't mean to cause trouble. The most annoying thing that she would do, however, was to constantly whine and complain about her sorry lot in life. All the girls who came into juvenile hall were experiencing one sort of crisis or another; no one wanted to hear all about Terry's problems.

The juvenile hall staff soon noticed that Terry was consuming all of the time in group sessions, either because she herself wanted to talk about her problems, or because the other girls wanted to talk about their anger toward her for being a "snitch." The staff decided that this situation was helpful neither for Terry nor the other girls. This assessment was communicated to the unit at a group meeting, and it was decided that the first five minutes of each future session would be set aside for Terry. During those five minutes she could talk about her complaints, or others could complain about her, but only five minutes would be devoted to Terry. During the day, if Terry started whining and complaining, she would be required to spend fifteen minutes of her recess or recreation time in her room thinking about her behavior. This system was set up not only to discourage this behavior but also to remind Terry when her behavior was unacceptable; her whining, complaining, and infantile behavior had become such a habit by now that she seemed unaware of what she was doing.

For a few days, it seemed that Terry lost more recreation and recess time than she had been granted. But at the end of two weeks, the staff noticed that none of the group's time was being spent on Terry, that she was no longer being kept in her room during recess, and that she had become involved in the recreation programs. She was behaving appropriately. Her parents, who came to the family group meeting, mentioned that Terry seemed so much better. She appeared less nervous and happier than she had been for a long time.

Terry, by this time, was bragging to the staff about her escapade of running away from home and about her stay in juvenile hall and seemed proud of being a "delinquent girl." She said that she had been teased a lot for having been in a mental hospital and for seeing a therapist. Now, on two separate occasions, girls from her school had been admitted to juvenile hall and, rather than teasing her, they seemed to accept her. Observing this, Terry tried all the more to learn to adapt her behavior so that she did not irritate people.

By the time she left the juvenile hall, Terry seemed much improved. Her behavior had been modified by the technique of structuring the amount of group session time that could be devoted to her and by sending her to her room to think about inappropriate behavior. The counseling by the psychiatrist and the juvenile hall staff helped her understand what behavior was inappropriate and how to behave differently. She came to think of herself as a "delinquent" girl who had been to juvenile hall. She exchanged her identity of being a neurotic girl who has problems and behaves in a peculiar manner for the identity of a delinquent girl. Being labeled delinquent is much more socially acceptable in some subcultures than being considered neurotic. Terry's parents found it much more comfortable to have a delinquent daughter than to have a neurotic daughter. Her parents became much more accepting of Terry when she stopped the behavior that had previously embarrassed them.

By the time Terry left the juvenile hall, she was talking about reforming. She announced that she intended to stop all her delinquent behavior. Although being away from home only once briefly and being caught the first time she tried to steal is not much of a delinquent past, it had been sufficient to allow Terry to consider herself delinquent. She decided she would try to stop running away and stealing. Having accepted the identity of a delinquent, she could now become a reformed delinquent. Since the identity of the adolescent girl is not as permanently established as that of the adult, she can more readily change. Normally, of course, one tries to avoid letting an adolescent come to see herself as delinquent. Hopefully, all adolescent girls will not need to go through a delinquent phase in order to improve, but in Terry's case this seemed helpful.

In the case of Rhonda, we see another teenage girl who, because of her behavior, developed an identity that caused her to become depressed. With the aid of psychotherapy, she was able to modify both her behavior and her identity. Rhonda, fourteen years old, was brought to the emergency room of a general hospital by her mother for having taken an overdose of sleeping pills. Although Rhonda took only five of the capsules, she claimed that she wanted to kill herself. Her mother, from whose room the medication was taken, was very concerned about her daughter's apparent suicide attempt. Rhonda was referred to a psychotherapist.

Rhonda was the second of four children. A freshman in high school, she was doing poorly in her classes and would take every opportunity to stay home from school. Her older sister, a senior at the continuation high school, had a similar distaste for school. She was employed part time in a clothing store and had a reputation in the neighborhood for sexual promiscuity. Neither girl's school problems particularly upset the mother. Rhonda also had an eleven-year-old sister who appeared to have no problems other than a similar disinterest for school. The youngest sibling, an eight-year-old brother, was described as being "all boy."

Her mother had divorced Rhonda's father several years before at the insistence of the three girls. The father had been unemployed, abused alcohol, beat his wife, and intimidated the children. The therapist felt that it was a bit unusual for the children in a family to insist that their parents divorce, but Rhonda and her mother both maintained that the divorce was the children's idea. Rhonda was not able to objectively assess anything her mother said or did; instead, she was very protective of her mother, who seemed to evoke a great deal of sympathy from her. Rhonda, for example, was still angry at her mother's former boss for having fired her three years earlier. Actually, she had been fired because she did not arrive on time and was not doing enough work. She had not sought employment since.

Rhonda's mother dated a man she referred to as her boyfriend. Occasionally he became involved in family activities and usually gave Rhonda and the other children gifts on birthdays and Christmas. Her mother also had several other male friends who fixed things around the house, bought groceries for the

family, or provided clothing for the children. The therapist assumed that the mother was sexually active with several of the men
who were helping her financially, but if this was suggested to
Rhonda, even tentatively, she would protest vigorously.

The mother arranged for Rhonda to have psychotherapy
once a week and to attend an adolescent activity center twice a
week. As the therapy progressed and her actions in the center
were observed, it appeared that Rhonda knew little about relating to other adolescents. Shy and embarrassed, she had difficulty
in talking with her peers. She knew very little about popular
music and did not know how to dance. She also seemed not to
know about the latest teenage fads and clothes and dressed instead in seductive clothing that looked too old for her. Although
she did not know how to play and joke with her peers, she could
be flirtatious with the boys at the adolescent center. Flirtatious-
ness seemed to be her only mode of relating.

In her conversations with the therapist, Rhonda described
some wild scenes in which boys from school dropped by her house
to drink and use drugs while her mother was away. Fights broke
out and girls were chased into the street. Although Rhonda
denied that she herself was sexually active, she said she was "on
the pill." She explained that her mother had taken her to a doctor
shortly after her menstrual periods started because she had experienced bad cramps. Birth control pills had been prescribed to
alleviate them. Eventually, Rhonda told the therapist that she
was, indeed, sexually active, and that she had taken the original
overdose because the boy down the block had refused to talk to
her at school the day after they had sex. This happened with
other boys also; they would not talk to her at school but would
come around to have sex with her after school. At those times,
they would be nice to her.

Rhonda used her time in the adolescent center to learn how
to relate to other teenagers. She eventually learned how to talk to
peers and to adults and began participating in teenage activities.
In her therapy hours, Rhonda discussed her embarrassment
about her home and family. The house had been condemned by
the health department, and her mother was not paying the rent.
As she was growing up, Rhonda was embarrassed by the sexual

activities of her mother and sister. Boys assumed that she was like her mother and sister, and she found herself sexually active before she had a chance to decide whether or not she wanted to be. Rhonda wanted to learn from the therapist how other teenage girls handled sex. She eventually decided she would not have sex with a boy unless there was a relationship between them. She stopped her sexual activity for some time and, as a result, came to feel less depressed and to believe that she was a good person. She found that she could decide when to have sex and that she was not required to do so with just any young man who happened to come over to her house.

In the meantime, however, the health department and the landlord had their way, and the family had to move. Rhonda now lived too far from the therapist to come for appointments. Both the therapist and Rhonda believed that she would do better in her new school than she had in the old. She saw it as a fresh chance to try out her recently acquired social skills.

Considering her case, we can observe that Rhonda acted out sexually before she had really made a conscious decision to do so. Her life circumstances obviously contributed to her behavior; everyone expected it of her. But, like so many disturbed younger adolescents, she still was behaving impulsively and without thought. She fell into a behavior pattern without deciding to do so. She did not allow herself time to learn how to relate to her peers or to decide what she wanted to do about her sexuality. Rhonda's identity changed as a result of her treatment: she came to see herself as being like other adolescent girls; she made plans for her future (she decided to enroll in a beauty school after high school); and she began to like herself better.

Rhonda's mother had come in for an initial interview with the therapist and had been in contact by phone several times. She brought Rhonda to the therapy sessions and thus overtly supported her daughter's treatment. However, Rhonda was able to overcome her depression without her mother's participation in psychotherapy, counseling, or conferences. If the mother's active participation in psychotherapy or counseling had been required for Rhonda's treatment, Rhonda would have had no treatment.

Not all of the younger adolescent girls who come to psychotherapy do so because of their impulsivity and their acting out. Although acting out may be a troublesome component of their behavior, depression may be the most urgent symptom. Depression in the younger adolescent is not apt to be the same type that one sees in the older girl or in the adult. The younger girl's depression, like her thinking, tends to be simplistic and concrete. Patients in this age group frequently have poor self-images because their parents think badly of them. For example, a girl may feel sad about the fact that she is no good — a fact that she accepts because her parents, especially her mother, says it is so. If her mother says she is a bad girl often enough and clearly enough, she must, in fact, be a bad girl. Her less formal and more simplistic thinking does not allow her to question this judgment or to wonder what caused it. She also does not think much about the future consequences of this self-concept.

Denise, fourteen-and-a-half years old, was sent to psychotherapy by her parents at the urging of the headmistress of a conservative girl's boarding school. In the initial telephone contact with the therapist, the headmistress stated that she was calling on behalf of the parents to start an evaluation process of Denise. Since the headmistress had been the one to suggest psychotherapy, the parents felt she could better explain the situation. She described herself as very strict and restrictive in her dealings with her charges but was concerned that Denise's parents were even stricter than herself, a situation which apparently amazed her.

Denise had been an only child until she started the seventh grade, when her younger sister was born. At about the same time, Denise's grades started falling off and she became interested in boys, much to her mother's consternation. Her mother supervised and checked up on her constantly and was overtly suspicious of Denise's relationship with her male acquaintances. One may conjecture that the time of her sister's birth was difficult for Denise. A surprise sibling can greatly trouble a young teenage girl. The arrival is undoubtedly an embarrassment because of the obvious implications that the parents are having sex. Many young teenage girls tend to see their parents as asexual. At any rate, being unable to control Denise to her satisfaction, the mother had sent her to the girls' boarding school. In addition, she structured all Denise's time away from school by sending her to camp during the summer and on supervised trips during spring break.

The family history, which was obtained partly from the parents and partly from Denise, revealed that her mother and father were married because her mother was pregnant with Denise. Her mother's attachment to her own mother was so strong that if she had not become pregnant she would have found it impossible to marry. The father had raised himself since leaving home at the age of fourteen. Working to support himself since then, he now owned his own business and was quite successful. He had left home after his mother's death and father's remarriage—a union that he could not tolerate. He essentially had no family until he married Denise's mother. Possibly because of their backgrounds, the parents were extremely close. They did everything together, made all decisions together, and went everywhere together; neither had any separate activities. The husband came home for lunch every day. This arrangement seemed satisfactory to both of them.

Denise complained of being depressed—or at least she thought she was depressed because the headmistress had said she was. She did know that she was unhappy. She complained of never being allowed to stay at home. She was always being sent away somewhere. The places she was sent to were nice, but why couldn't she ever just stay home? She felt that all these arrangements for sending her away from home indicated that she was bad. Her mother didn't trust her, therefore she knew she was bad and untrustworthy. Nonetheless she was homesick and wanted to live with her family. Wouldn't they ever forgive her?

It appeared that her mother was frightened by Denise's awakening sexual impulses and felt it her job to keep constant surveillance to be sure Denise did not get pregnant as she had. It is also possible that the closeness between the parents left no room for Denise; they were happy to be together without Denise's interference. This may have contributed to their desire to keep Denise away. The girl seemed to accept her parent's appraisal of her as someone bad and suspect. After all, they were her parents, and they ought to know. Also, she may have feared that her awakening sexual impulses were indeed bad and dangerous.

Office psychotherapy was recommended for Denise, and her parents agreed. The therapist also suggested that they keep Denise at home during summer vacation, ostensibly to allow her to continue psychotherapy. Denise's parents could not have tolerated a clear recommendation to let their daughter remain at home for the summer because she needed them. Such a statement would imply that they had erred as parents; they would have refused to accept this implication, but they did accept the face-saving compromise. The parents followed the recommendations. Denise came to therapy regularly for the rest of the school year and summer vacation. She talked a great deal of her homesickness and of her mother's suspiciousness. She also spoke of her interest in boys and of one counselor in particular, whom she had had a crush on for a year. She had told no one of her interest in this young man, nor was she open to hearing about the crushes of other girls; such interests, she believed, were suspect and frightening. Thus she did not realize that other teenagers have similar experiences and was fearful that this was but another indication of her "badness." Allowing her to talk about this young man and the other boys whom she was interested in was helpful, since the therapist did not react with horror as her mother might have.

Staying at home for the summer went well, and her parents decided to enroll her as a day student for the following year. Her mother appeared to be somewhat less fearful of Denise's interest in boys. In the psychotherapy sessions, Denise continued to complain that her mother did not trust her, but her self-esteem was better, and she was less depressed. Instead, she was now perplexed.

Prior to the psychotherapy Denise saw her mother as good and herself as bad; her mother saw it that way also. Now, as Denise began to change her impression of herself and gained more self-esteem, she began to wonder whether her mother might be bad or have serious problems. Denise seemed to sense that it would be dangerous for her to conclude that her mother was wrong or bad. If she were to accuse her mother of sending her away for her own neurotic reasons, her mother might do so again. Eventually, Denise decided that her mother was just overprotective. For Denise, this was an effective compromise. Some of her friends had overprotective mothers, and Denise stated that she could tolerate the situation at least until she was eighteen and ready to leave home.

In Denise's case, we have an example of the simplistic type of depression often found in younger adolescent girls. If her mother says she is bad, then it must be so. Was she good or was she bad as her mother said she was? Denise was not yet sufficiently separated from her mother to make such an evaluation on her own. We also see that both the patient and the therapist settled for easing Denise's depression and changing her self-esteem. No attempt was made to change the interaction or pathology of the whole family; no one, except Denise, would have accepted therapy for him- or herself. Denise was able to change her presenting symptom without her family changing at all. It was as if Denise had just one problem. How could she get along with her family as it was? Although one might conclude that greater intervention could have helped Denise even more, there might not have been any therapy at all if the therapist's goals had been set any higher.

Rosita was another young teenage girl with a depression directly related to her mother's telling her that she was worthless. Rosita had just turned fourteen when she was referred for therapy by a psychiatrist from an emergency room where she had been taken after swallowing a handful of sleeping pills while already intoxicated from alcohol. The act was impulsive and dangerous, as if she were tempting fate; it was not a planned suicide attempt. She was treated in the emergency room but not hospitalized. For six months prior to that overdose, Rosita had led a rather wild life with much drinking and partying. She had driven cars while unlicensed and intoxicated and had often jumped her horse fearlessly, suffering many falls and a knee operation as a result. She complained of feeling depressed and had suicidal thoughts when drinking. Her actions sounded very self-destructive. She said she was depressed because she could not stop fighting with her mother. She said she yelled at her mother all the time and hated herself because she could not stop.

In an initial interview with Rosita's mother, the woman said that her husband was an airline pilot and deliberately added that she was an ex-beauty pageant queen. Rosita was the youngest of her two children. Her son drank a lot and did not seem to be making much of his life. He had graduated from high school one year earlier. The boy's behavior did not seem to concern his mother. After complaining a great deal about Rosita's behavior, the mother went on to describe her anger toward her daughter. As she talked more, it became apparent that some of her actions toward her daughter were almost sadistic. She would promise Rosita some new clothing and then change her mind because Rosita was "no good." She redecorated the whole house with the exception of Rosita's room, for which she would not even buy a new bedspread. Rosita later complained that her bedspread really was in bad condition. In conversations with the therapist, the mother could only express anger toward Rosita and no concern for her safety. Her anger was unrelenting.

In the course of her psychotherapy, Rosita became quite dependent on the therapist. She appreciated the attention she was receiving — attention seemed to be something she was deprived of. She reported a good relationship with her mother until she reached adolescence; then her mother seemed to be always angry with her and Rosita could do nothing to appease her. The girl talked of being a bad person and felt that this was the reason for her mother's behavior toward her. She talked of wanting to die and about instances when she tried to get herself killed but failed. She thought of suicide but wanted to die in such a way as to make it look like an accident. She had suicidal thoughts mostly when drinking.

The therapist frequently confronted Rosita with the inappropriateness of her poor self-image. As a result, she slowly came to see that her mother was wrong about her, that her mother had taken every opportunity to berate and degrade her, and that her poor self-image and poor self-esteem were the result. As Rosita began to feel that she was not such a bad person, her behavior improved. She became less depressed and her self-destructive episodes stopped.

With new insight into how her mother had helped her to feel so badly about herself, Rosita tried to live at home and to ignore her mother's attempts to scold her. The girl tried not to let her mother provoke her into yelling and fighting, but the situation was difficult both for Rosita and her parents. Eventually, the therapist recommended sending her to a school in a distant city—one which her father could visit in the course of his work but which her mother could not, because of her many duties at home. Since this suggestion was agreeable to all, arrangements were made.

Rosita now saw the therapist only rarely. Her last visits occurred after her graduation, after her marriage, and just after the birth of her first child. She had married a man who was in the navy, and she hoped that a letter from the therapist attesting to her previous psychotherapy would help to get her husband stationed near home. Aside from being too dependent on her husband, she looked well and happy and seemed to have a good marriage.

Rosita's mother was a narcissistic woman who apparently had great difficulty seeing her daughter grow into a young, attractive woman. The anger she directed toward Rosita was causing the girl to become depressed and to think badly of herself. Yet, the mother was actually very supportive of Rosita's therapy; she paid for it and frequently brought Rosita to her appointments. I assume, therefore, that she really did care what happened to her daughter but could not control her anger. However, she never came close to accepting any responsibility for Rosita's problem.

Rosita developed the type of depression so often seen in younger adolescent girls. Because they have not separated enough from their mothers, they are not able to assess for themselves the accuracy of their mothers' communication that they are bad. Girls who accept this judgment usually become depressed and, as was the case with Rosita, even self-destructive. Psychotherapy was helpful in giving Rosita an opportunity to see that she was not the bad girl her mother had led her to believe she was.

In the course of Rosita's treatment, the therapist was very active and did a great deal of the talking, especially when confronting her with the inappropriateness of her self-concept. The therapist told Rosita repeatedly that they both must try to determine why she regarded herself in such a bad light. Later, the therapist helped Rosita to understand that her low self-esteem was caused in large measure by her mother's tirades. When it became apparent.that the mother could not tolerate her daughter's presence, Rosita was advised to leave home for a period of time. These are, indeed, very active moves for a psychotherapist, but it seemed important that the therapist take action to prevent the girl from harming herself in one of her depressed, suicidal moods. An active therapist is frequently necessary when the patient is an adolescent girl.

Occasionally, a therapist working with girls in the earlier phase of adolescence will see a girl who suddenly develops a case of school phobia or school refusal. This school refusal with its fear of being in school often starts after a prolonged but vague illness, such as flu or infectious mononucleosis. Typically, the girl remains at home for a few weeks while she recovers but then refuses to return when well. Usually this type of situation occurs with "good" girls, who never tried to skip school before, never got into any trouble, and are close to their mothers.

When one sees a case of abrupt school fear, one would do well to look into the mother's psychological situation. Sometimes a younger adolescent girl remains so attached to her mother that the two are almost psychologically fused. The daughter may react to her mother's depression by developing symptoms that require her to remain at home, keeping her mother company. Neither mother nor daughter may be aware of what is happening.

In such cases, it is important to try to get the girl back to school before the mother's overdependence on her daughter becomes irreversible and before the girl's fear of returning becomes greater. Sometimes, the school is willing to send work home to prevent the girl from falling too far behind, making the return easier. Sometimes allowing the girl to attend for just as long as she can, with mother waiting by the phone, prepared to collect her should the panic become intolerable, makes it easier for her to return. This technique allows the girl to feel that she is still in contact with her mother.

This method was employed with success in the case of Mary. With her mother's help, Mary quickly caught up on her work and returned to school. She was assured that her mother would be at home near the phone should she need her. She called her mother and was picked up frequently during the first week or so, but then settled for telephone contact or for her mother coming to school to see her; after such a visit, Mary could return to her classes.

At the time of this episode, Mary was a thirteen-year-old enrolled in junior high school. She was the youngest of three girls: the eldest was married and living away from home and the other, who was working, would probably be leaving home soon. The mother was a widow, living on a small railroad pension, who took in laundry to supplement her income. She had been widowed for many years and had never remarried or even dated another man.

Although Mary refused to go to school, saying she was very frightened, she otherwise appeared to be fairly outgoing, friendly, and rather enterprising. For example, she earned money by cutting apricots, mowing lawns, and babysitting. She was well liked in the neighborhood. The family was respected for their efforts to manage well despite the small pension on which they lived. Mary had no fear of going into neighborhood houses or of walking around in the hills, which she dearly loved to do, yet she seemed to panic at even the thought of going to school.

The mother, in contrast to Mary's affable, friendly attitude, looked and acted quite depressed. She complained of insomnia, lacked the energy to do her chores, and seemed desperate to talk with the therapist alone. She cried when confronted with the fact that she appeared depressed. The mother was a proud woman who never could have brought herself to therapy, but now that she had the opportunity, she readily talked about her sense of loss: her husband was dead and her girls would soon be leaving home. She talked about how she still missed her husband and resented him for dying. Yet she felt that her resentment was wrong, since he clearly could not help dying, and he had been such a good husband. It appeared that the mother needed counseling more than Mary, and she agreed to come in and talk with the therapist alone for a series of interviews, ostensibly to help her daughter. Mary's mother would never have allowed herself to spend money to help herself, but she was quite willing to pay to help her daughter.

During the course of these interviews, some of the mother's involutional concerns, such as her daughters growing up and leaving, were discussed, as was her still-unresolved grief for her husband. Her depression improved rapidly. For a small part of each hour, she talked about Mary's progress and her going to school to reassure Mary that she was all right. She felt compelled to talk about Mary for at least a few minutes to prevent feeling guilty about coming for help herself. The mother very early became aware of the meaning of her daughter's illness: Mary stayed at home to make sure that her mother was all right.

Because of financial difficulties, the mother could not come in for therapy regularly and Mary was rarely seen. Mary's mother had refused a clinic referral from the outset because she wanted only the best for her daughter and believed that the psychotherapy would be better if it cost more. She agreed to send ten dollars a month until she paid her bill, and she did exactly that.

When a psychotherapist sees a case of school fear or school refusal in a young adolescent girl who is very attached to her mother, the therapist would do well to determine whether or not the mother is depressed. Some younger girls are so attached to their parents that they seem to know, almost intuitively, when their parent needs them to be nearby.

From the cases cited in this chapter, one can see that a girl in the earlier phase of adolescence can be helped by psychotherapy. The treatment process is facilitated by the girl's need for attention and by her need to obtain approval from an adult. In the therapy relationship, she is likely to become very dependent on her therapist. A great deal of patience and a protective attitude on the part of the therapist are crucial because the younger adolescent is basically so vulnerable — she is so easily damaged by her own impulses and by what her parents think of her. For these reasons, manipulating her environment may be as important as offering direct support.

THREE

Limit Setting on the Younger Adolescent

The acting-out, impulsive, defiant, younger adolescent girl, who resists psychotherapy to the limit and questions its value, is the girl who makes the psychotherapist feel that he or she has a tiger by the tail. By their behavior some of these adolescents are clearly asking for someone— their parents, their psychotherapist, or some other adult in authority—to set limits on their acting out or parameters within which they must confine their behavior. Frequently, their acting out is provocative and so inviting of intervention that they obviously do not want to behave as they do.

Many adolescents experiment: They want to see what happens if they do not come home at night when expected and how people react if they associate with adolescents from a different subculture. Or they will try street drugs just to feel their reaction. This type of considered experimentation is not what is referred to here. The acting-out, defiant adolescent is, for example, the fourteen-year-old girl who smokes marijuana only when already so intoxicated that she can hardly walk, while she is out on the streets, and in the presence of a uniformed police officer; almost invariably she gets caught. This kind of behavior is so provocative that it invites intervention by an adult; the adolescent is asking to be stopped.

When a youngster of this type comes in for treatment, the therapist must first supply the limits the adolescent is asking for and then try to determine what the adolescent is attempting to say by her behavior. Through acting out, many adolescents are saying that they feel as if they were moving too quickly toward adulthood. They feel out of control, as if they were in a car going downhill without brakes. They see adulthood, freedom, decision making, and the responsibility for resisting the temptations of the world as too much for them to handle.

Some adolescents, fearful that they will never be able to leave their parents' side or face the challenges of the world, plunge into all sorts of frightening situations in a counterphobic manner. By doing so, they deny their fear. The adolescent girl who grew up fearful and protected may suddenly start going wherever and whenever she pleases without feeling fear. Although she may have previously experienced fear of sex and men, she now behaves counterphobically, going with any man and having sex with anyone she chooses. But her behavior may be so defiant and flagrant that it invites intervention. Other adolescents may use their behavior to cry out for help with a family problem. If the problem interferes with her separation from her family, the adolescent may act out in a manner that invites intervention. One of her parents, for example, may be trying to keep her dependent and at home for his or her own neurotic reasons. Or perhaps the girl is being used to hold her parents' marriage together. Every time she tries to become a bit more independent, they threaten to separate. Feeling guilty, she may try to patch up the argument between them. If all else fails, her wild acting out may temporarily unite them in concern for her. Sometimes, a girl who has been too close to her father may feel that by separating, she is abandoning him and causing him to be depressed. Her acting out may provide enough excitement to distract her from her worry and guilt over her father. The reasons for an adolescent's cry for help will vary. The task of the psychotherapist is to determine why she is calling for help, but first the behavior must be stopped or at least slowed down enough to allow it to be analyzed.

Miller (1974) states that the adolescent does not seem to develop a fairly circumscribed neurotic symptom to indicate that there is a problem to be solved but instead shows a more generalized personality problem. He describes an important distinction between the neurosis seen in an adult, which can be found in an otherwise healthy personality, and the neurosis of the adolescent, which always implies, according to Miller, a general personality impairment. He adds that all therapeutic and parenting moves should involve attempts to strengthen the general personality. By first setting some limits and slowing down the acting-out behavior, then trying to help the adolescent understand her conflicts, and lastly helping her to handle her fears and problems, the psychotherapist helps to strengthen the adolescent girl's personality.

Many of the younger girls who have difficulty handling their impulses and managing their behavior will allow the psychotherapist to supply the limits they need. After tolerating these external controls for a time, the adolescent will often try to limit her own behavior because her therapist wants her to and she wants to please her therapist. Eventually, the girl comes to limit her own behavior because she herself wants to. At that point, the girl may even tell her psychotherapist that it was her idea to behave appropriately from the beginning. She has incorporated the limits and now considers them her own.

A psychiatrist who had much experience treating adolescent girls, but who had never been inside a juvenile hall before, decided to visit the institution before starting to work there. On that day she had lunch in one of the units. Seated at a table with nine girls and no other adults, she carried on a superficial conversation. She asked the girls what they had done in school that morning and where they were from; the girls in turn asked her what a psychiatrist did and how long one had to go to school to become one. The girls and the staff seemed to be observing the psychiatrist very closely to see whether or not she would "fit in." When it came time for dessert, there was a great deal of activity as the girls dished out some canned peaches and passed them around. This done, the psychiatrist discovered that, in the flurry of passing around the dishes, her dessert was missing. She insisted that everyone stop eating immediately and look for the lost dessert. Someone found it and the meal resumed.

While there were undoubtedly other times when she was tested by the girls, this introduction apparently went quite well. Many of the girls trusted her. They felt that she understood them. The psychiatrist showed the girls that she could recognize, tolerate, and deal with acting-out behavior. A psychotherapist treating adolescent girls in private practice must do the same.

Sometimes, by force of personality alone, the therapist can set limits on the acting out of the younger adolescent girl in treatment. If the therapist says such things as, "No, that is not one of your options!" or "I don't want you to do that!" or "You know that you can't do that!" the acting out can sometimes be deterred. If the therapist insists, unequivocally, that he or she does not want the younger adolescent to behave self-destructively, this will often be effective in setting limits on the girl's behavior. Of course, firmness of this sort does not always work, and the psychotherapist may need to explore other methods of setting limits.

If the girl is being seen as an outpatient, the therapist may need to join forces with her parents to find ways of limiting her behavior. Despite the fact that her therapist is clearly involved in the limit-setting process, the younger adolescent does not seem to find it difficult to relate to the psychotherapist. If her acting out is really out of control, she will need and appreciate the limits. There may, or course, be an initial show of anger.

When I speak of setting limits on the adolescent's behavior, I am not implying that strong force should be used to stop every bit of acting out or undesirable behavior. Complete control of the adolescent's impulses would hardly help her learn to handle these by herself. In his essay on juvenile courts, Aichorn ([1925] 1964) makes a clear distinction between suppression and restriction of impulses. He believes that restricting the impulses only to the degree necessary will help the adolescent shape these instinctual demands into a socially acceptable form. Limit setting on the adolescent's behavior should strive only for such necessary restriction and not complete suppression of the impulses.

In the next case, the mother when too far in her attempts to suppress her daughter's impulses and thus became too rejecting of her. Peggy was the fourth of five children. She had three older sisters living away from home, two of whom were married. She and a younger brother lived with the parents. Peggy's acting out came to her parents' attention following a dinner at the home of some family friends. After the meal, the adults decided to play bridge while Peggy's brother played with the hosts' son. Peggy was bored and wandered about the house. She stole a baby bracelet and a watch from the hosts' bedroom. Several days later, the hostess called Peggy's mother to tell her that the bracelet and watch were missing, and that she suspected Peggy of having taken them. Finding that this was indeed the case, Peggy's mother was horrified. After returning the stolen items with an apology, Peggy was "grounded"—she was allowed no social activities and no phone calls. Peggy accepted this punishment, but her mother was still concerned, embarrassed, and very angry. She decided to bring Peggy in for counseling and to seek advice on how to handle her.

The first two sessions were joint interviews with Peggy and her mother both talking with the therapist. Peggy agreed that she should not have taken the things. She explained that she had been bored and angry. The two families did a lot of socializing, and whenever they were together, everyone else seemed to have someone to do things with except Peggy. She felt left out. The adults liked to play bridge and were always very absorbed in their game; the two boys enjoyed each other's company. Peggy wished she could stay at home when the family visited their friends, but her mother never allowed this. She felt that since Peggy was only fourteen years old she should not stay at home alone.

Her mother said that she was unable to overcome her anger with Peggy; she had been too embarrassed. She could not understand how a daughter of hers could have so little conscience. She herself had always had a very strict conscience, and it was impossible for her to understand how Peggy could steal anything.

Peggy complained that ever since the incident, her mother was constantly angry with her. They could not talk without her mother criticizing her repeatedly. Peggy said that she could tolerate the punishment and even felt she deserved it, but she could not tolerate her mother's anger toward her. When would her mother stop? She said she was beginning to feel very guilty. Even before the incident, Peggy complained, her mother rarely acted nice to her or gave her much companionship. She wondered if her mother even liked her.

The mother said she was aware that Peggy wanted her to be different. She knew that Peggy wanted a warm, giving mother who could provide a great deal of companionship, but she was not that type of person. The mother described herself as efficient, abrupt, and strict—but fair. She said she had never really enjoyed any of her children except when they were babies. She tried to do the right things for Peggy, as she had for the others, but she was looking forward to the time when all the children were grown and she and her husband could enjoy each other's company alone.

The therapist told the mother that she had acted wisely in punishing Peggy for the theft, but that her persistent anger with her might cause her to act out more. If the therapist had not condoned the mother's basic childrearing philosophy, the therapist's credibility with Peggy's mother would have been lost. The therapist also suggested that the mother's excessive anger appeared to come from her own guilt and fears that she might not be a good mother. If she could stop feeling so guilty, then she might be able to stop feeling so angry with Peggy. This would also free the mother to cope with the present problem. Peggy's mother took that advice and apparently began feeling less guilty. If the therapist did not think she was terrible, perhaps she was not. As a result, things started to improve around the house. Peggy was still grounded, but somehow she and her mother were becoming a little closer. Peggy no longer complained that her mother spent all her time playing bridge or golf or that she was not buying her the clothes she needed.

Peggy's mother had apparently been so alarmed by her daughter's behavior that she started putting tremendous pressure on her to ensure that Peggy did not steal again. She was trying to suppress her daughter's impulses and drives completely. With the aid of counseling, however, she became aware that her behavior was caused by her own guilt. As a result, she was able to modify her anger toward her daughter. The mother gave Peggy some of the love the girl wanted, which, in addition to the limit setting, proved effective in dissuading her from stealing.

The case of Peggy illustrates the difference between attempting to completely suppress an adolescent's impulses and applying the right amount of force to restrict them. Peggy's mother was so horrified by her daughter's behavior that she tried to totally suppress Peggy's urge to steal. Yet stealing is a ubiquitous urge one must learn to cope with, as Peggy needed to do. In this case we also see the value of direct advice given to a parent. Peggy's mother felt so guilty about rearing a child who could steal that she might have ruminated forever about her inadequacies and failings as a mother if the therapist had not stopped her.

Some parents find it difficult to believe that one of their children needs a great deal of limit setting while the others do not. Unaccustomed to setting limits, they may find it difficult to understand why one daughter will act less responsibly than her siblings, even as she presses for more and more privileges. They do not understand why they are always being put in the position of having to say no. Yet by not setting appropriate limits, they give their daughter license to act out. All children do not need the same type of parenting. One adolescent, unable to handle her own impulses and drives, may need much more parental structure to do so, while the other children in the same family need much less. By setting appropriate limits on their daughter's behavior, parents can give her the parental structure she needs.

While we can sympathize with the parents who are confused because they are continually having to say no to just one child, it is difficult to understand parents who never wish to set any limits on their children's behavior for fear of appearing authoritarian and overbearing. When it becomes necessary for such indulgent parents to bring their daughter in for psychotherapy, they are perplexed as to why their daughter is so rebellious and out of control. They describe their attempts to be modern, enlightened parents and to avoid being authoritarian and inhibiting as their own parents had been. What went wrong? Why is she so unhappy and defiant? What more could they have done? They tried to give her everything she wanted.

Holmes (1964) put it aptly when he said, "At the extreme of the benevolence-malevolence continuum is the exhaustively over-indulgent, overprotective parent who, by withholding all visible forms of punishment or discipline, inflicts the cruelest punishment of all. He teaches his child nothing about reality" (p.15). Holmes feels that "Children need to react against reasonable standards of behavior set down by their parents and therapists alike so that the adolescent can determine his own reality" (p. 15).

Cindy's parents avoided disciplining and punishing their daughter. By doing do, they failed to give her the parental support and structure she needed. Cindy was a "hard-acting," abrasive, fifteen-year-old, hospitalized for having made a suicide gesture with an overdose of pills. While at the hospital she disrupted ward routines, coming and going whenever she pleased in the open adult psychiatric ward. She also persuaded other young patients to join her in acting up. She left the ward to smoke marijuana or take LSD on one or two occasions, and she protested all attempts to help her, saying she was not crazy and did not belong in a mental hospital. Yet, when her psychiatrist wished to discharge her, she refused to leave.

Cindy's behavior was intolerable to the nursing staff. When asked by a nurse how she was feeling or what upset her, she would reply with profanities and protest, "Why should I tell you? You are supposed to help me, aren't you? Aren't you one of the normal ones who knows *all* the answers?" When invited to participate in a group therapy session or group recreational activities, Cindy refused to do "that dumb thing! What's that supposed to do for me anyway?" She constantly berated her therapist, whom she learned was going through a divorce, and yelled at him for leaving his wife. She made sure to tell all of her therapist's other patients about his divorce and how terrible he was. She stayed awake at night disturbing the other patients and slept during the day, cursing anyone who tried to awaken her. She refused to talk with her parents when they visited and refused to leave the hospital when her therapist suggested she be discharged. Cindy did, however, leave the hospital whenever she wished, any time of the day or night, to ride away on her motorcycle and return when she wanted.

Eventually, the ward chief suggested to Cindy's therapist that he call in someone else to treat her. He suggested that Cindy might respond better to a female therapist and one was contacted immediately. After meeting with the parents first, to determine whether or not she had their support, the psychotherapist went to the hospital to meet Cindy. She introduced herself as her new therapist, hired by her parents to work with her. Cindy protested very strongly, saying that she did not want the woman as her "shrink" and that she was going to fire her just as quickly as she had been hired. The psychiatrist indicated that Cindy did not have that option, being a minor and all. Cindy replied that she hated her and did not intend to cooperate. The psychotherapist replied, "I tend to grow on people. Perhaps you will come to like me." Cindy's answer to this was, "You grow on people! Like a fungus?" Ignoring this rudeness, the psychotherapist said that they were going to start by restricting Cindy to the ward unless she was accompanied by a member of the nursing staff. Also, the psychiatrist was going to call her parents and tell them to come to the hospital to pick up her motorcycle, since she had no need for it at this time.

Of course, Cindy protested all this vigorously, but it happened nonetheless. She allowed her therapist to set these limits on her behavior. There was no way that her therapist could have enforced these rules in an open hospital setting. Cindy could have just walked off. She must have wanted some limits, or perhaps she had never been confronted before by anyone in authority who did not get angry but sounded like she really meant what she said.

As the therapist came to grow on Cindy, the girl told her about her intense fears, which she had told no one about before. She explained that she was afraid to be at home alone when her parents were out. She sat on the sofa all night and imagined that the floor and carpet about her were a sea of burning fire. She could convince herself that was true and that she must not step on the floor for fear that her feet might really burn. She sat on the sofa all night with her feet tucked under her, watching, waiting, and afraid. In addition, she was afraid of the dark and afraid to go almost anywhere at night and embarrassed to tell anyone of her fears. She was also worried that she might lose her boyfriend, whom she hated, loved, feared, and wanted all at the same time. Cindy remained in the hospital for two weeks under the supervision of her new therapist. Gradually permitted more privileges, she reluctantly began to participate in hospital activities with the other patients. When Cindy felt that her impulsiveness was under control, that the therapist was in charge of her life, and that she was very dependent on the therapist, she was comfortable enough to allow herself to be discharged. She returned home and continued with office visits to the same therapist.

During the course of psychotherapy, this fifteen-year-old girl struggled valiantly to keep from becoming too dependent on her therapist by trying to miss appointments. At the same time, however, she spent hours sketching intricate pictures to illustrate how she felt or writing long notes to explain herself and her fears and slipped them under the therapist's office door during the night. The therapist provided a rationalization that helped ease Cindy's fear of dependency by indicating that Cindy was like a boxer with a trainer in her corner who could help, but she still had to fight the fight alone. This rationalization seemed to relieve Cindy's fear.

On several occasions in the course of therapy, Cindy's parents were encouraged to set limits on their daughter's behavior. They were able to do this with the support of the therapist. For example, early in the therapy the parents were encouraged to stop allowing Cindy to have sex with her boyfriend in her room. Cindy's thirteen-year-old brother was delighted with this change. He had been too embarrassed for months to bring his friends home because of the noises coming from the bedroom. On another occasion, about midway through her therapy, Cindy left home for two days and nights and was found sleeping in a wooded park. Her parents were encouraged to ask the police who found Cindy to take her to a juvenile hall instead of bringing her directly home. They were also advised not to be in too much of a hurry to pick her up the next day. They did just that and were proud that they had the strength to do so. In their pride, Cindy's parents felt compelled to tell her that they had requested her admission to the juvenile hall. On learning this, Cindy said, "I didn't know you cared about me that much." Apparently, she had assumed that their prior lack of limit setting was due to disinterest in her. She was also surprised to learn that there were so many dangers in the world. She had heard frightening tales from the other girls in the juvenile hall. This was interesting—she was now talking about real dangers in the world and not about her imaginary fears.

Eventually, Cindy began discussing her relationship with her mother, a woman she found difficult to live with but difficult to separate from. She complained about her mother's inconsistencies, unpredictable rages, and hypocrisy. Because of her mother's long-standing habit of being unpredictable and inconsistent, Cindy had failed to develop the sense of inner security that would have allowed her to become gradually independent. The woman's failure to support her daughter by setting limits on her acting out also contributed to the girl's crippling anxieties. Although she found it difficult to do so, Cindy managed to live at home in relative peace until she went away to college.

Cindy went to a little college that she described as being snuggled in a valley surrounded by protective mountains; from her description, the college sounded like a protected haven. She really was not the "hard," abrasive, independent girl she had originally tried to portray. The therapist's last contact from Cindy was an invitation to her wedding. She was marrying a young man from school and was doing well without psychotherapy. She added that she still had her motorcycle.

Cindy's main conflict was an independence-dependence struggle. She was grasping for freedom and independence without acknowledging that she had any dependency needs. She claimed she did not need her mother and hoped she was not like her. Cindy was her own person—or so she thought. Cindy had rushed toward freedom and independence in a counterphobic manner. She was fearful of leaving her parents. She was so dependent on her mother that she could not stay at home alone without becoming fearful. Cindy needed to be allowed freedom and independence in titrated amounts, amounts she could handle. But first she had to be stopped. When her parents and her psychotherapist cooperated in setting limits on her behavior, she became less anxious. Her parents had previously been very indulgent with Cindy. She had told them that she could manage her own life, and they believed her. By not stopping her from acting out, they did not give her the support she needed.

Barbara was another adolescent girl whose provocative behavior seemed to invite intervention. Her acting out appeared to be in response to a family problem. Barbara was fifteen years old and had one sibling, a younger brother. With her famliy, she had moved to the area about six months earlier, following her father's retirement from the military. The family had moved many times before because of the father's military career, and both children seemed to have adjusted to these moves fairly well. Barbara, who always did well in school and seemed to find friends immediately, had taken these transitions especially easily. She had been dating since the age of thirteen, and her father proudly talked of Barbara's popularity with the boys. Even though they had moved many times, she had always been asked to school proms and special dances.

Now, however, Barbara was doing very poorly in school. Notices were being sent home about her incomplete work and her absenteeism. Two times recently, she had been suspended from school for cutting classes. In a conference with the school psychologist, Barbara's parents learned that she had been signing her mother's name to excuses for absence. When asked about this, Barbara told her parents that it was none of their business and wondered what they intended to do about it. She warned them that if they stopped her from forging the excuses, she would only be suspended again because she intended to continue cutting classes whenever she wanted.

Barbara would not come home at night at the time she was told to and would give her parents no explanations for returning late. Several times her father had caught her sneaking out of the window at night to meet a boy—and it was not always the same boy. She was irritable and berated her parents so strongly when they asked her what was happening that they became afraid to ask. In a conference at school, Barbara did not talk to the counselor but just pointed to her father and accused him of being the problem, much to her father's embarrassment.

The school psychologist referred Barbara and her parents to a psychotherapist for an evaluation. Barbara refused to see a therapist because she saw no need. She told her parents to go instead since they needed the help, not she. She said that if she were forced to go she would not talk at all and that it would be a waste of time. The father felt that psychotherapy could not help because of his daughter's attitude, but he found from reading her diary that she was plagued with suicidal thoughts. He decided to bring her to the therapist even if she protested.

The first session consisted of a joint interview with Barbara and her parents. The father did most of the talking, describing the behavioral problems, while Barbara just sulked. She was making an obvious display of not talking, as she had promised to do. Near the end of the session, the therapist, with Barbara present, said that for the next few months Barbara would need to have a great deal more structure in her life than she previously had. The mother was to drive Barbara to school every day and make sure that Barbara actually went in the door. Barbara's father was to meet with the school counselor and arrange for Barbara to bring home weekly progress reports from each teacher. The school would be asked to call her mother immediately if Barbara missed a class. Barbara protested this plan, but she seemed more amazed than anything else. It was hard for her to object too much when she had told her parents ahead of time that she did not intend to talk. The plan of adding structure was effective — except for a few instances of testing out the limits, the whole family cooperated. At one point, Barbara left her father this note:

> Dear Sir:
>
> The above is purely a mark of respect, for that is all I have left for you. I can't even hate you — there is just a lack of feeling.
>
> Thank you for giving me my life and for all the opportunities and advantages you have given me. I can never repay you for that. But I cannot thank you for the love that is not there. . . .
>
> The psychotherapist is of great beneficial help. How-

ever, you have far greater need of one than I, "your neurotic daughter" do!

Perhaps in less than a year we shall both regret what we have said and written. Who can say?

Once I was proud of you—at your retirement parade. When you took me out to dinner. When you were a big deal distinguished officer serving his country.

Now you are one of millions. . . . Give me nothing for Christmas or birthdays or graduation. You are incapable of loving—so give nothing and you will receive nothing.

Thank you for all you've done.

I respect you, yes, but have a lack of other feelings for you, past, present, and/or future and I am *not* failing *all* my subjects and I'm *glad* I humiliated you.

Ever unfortunately yours,

Barbara

This note upset her father as it was intended to do. He brought the note to the psychotherapist and said that he was also upset that Barbara had removed his picture from her bureau. She had always kept this picture of him, which had been taken when he was twenty years old, in her bedroom. The father, weakening under Barbara's pressure, had come to see the therapist to ask that the plan of structuring Barbara's life be stopped. Although this apparent rejection was very painful for him, the father was convinced by the therapist that it was still necessary to structure Barbara's life.

In her therapy sessions, Barbara complained of her father's unrealistic expectations of her. He expected her to be a top student in high school, to go to college, and to become someone great. She knew she could pass all her subjects, but she also knew that she was an average student and that she was not interested in going to college. She explained that her father had always thought of her as being adorable and that he expected her to be very popular—an expectation Barbara tried to live up to. The reason she was asked out so much was that she usually had sex with her dates. Her father, she said, never figured out how she could be so popular so quickly after they moved to a new area. But now,

Barbara's secret to instant popularity was not working. She did meet young men quickly and did have sex with them, but boys were no longer taking her to the prom or on fancy dinner dates. Young men were not proud to be seen with her.

Barbara was depressed, and her acting out was a cry for help. Her sexual activity, she thought, was a product of her father's wish for her to be desirable; her father did indeed wish this. At the same time, however, he found Barbara very attractive himself and related to her in a very seductive manner. This close relationship between Barbara and her father may have been too intense for Barbara to handle now that she was physically mature. Her sexual escapades diverted her thoughts from her father. If there is a strong mother in the family, the closeness between a father and his teenage daughter is easier for both to tolerate. It is as if the mother will make sure that there is only fantasy and no action. Barbara's mother, however, was a pleasant but nonassertive woman who made no decisions or suggestions in the family; she just seemed to tag along. Barbara's sexual activity appeared to be both an escape from the intensity of her closeness to her father and a retaliation designed to embarrass him.

The therapist's strong stand in prescribing roles for the girl and her parents was very helpful in easing Barbara's fears over her relationship with her father; someone outside was now in charge of the family and in charge of her behavior. Barbara could relax and go about her task of maturing, finding her identity, and learning to cope with her problems. She did just that, using her therapy hours to discuss her problems with school, males, and the future. The external controls were not needed very long. Her visits with the therapist gave her the feeling of protection she needed and the opportunity to develop the sense of mastery she wanted. She improved fairly rapidly.

In both of the cases discussed earlier, the girls were depressed and had identity problems, which needed to be worked out in psychotherapy. One of the tasks of the treatment was to gain some understanding of the reasons for the depression, but greater emphasis was placed on helping these adolescents master the fears and problems they faced. But psychotherapy could not have proceeded in either case without first setting limits on the girl's behavior. These were set firmly, calmly, and unambivalently. Although the therapist was clearly involved in the limit setting, the atmosphere of confidence and confidentiality was maintained in the psychotherapy sessions. The girl in the earlier phase of adolescence may not like limits, but she appreciates them when they are necessary.

It is important for the therapist to decide before setting limits whether or not he or she will be able to carry out the plan. It can be very embarrassing — and even antitherapeutic — to tell a girl that she is going to be stopped from behaving in a self-destructive manner, and then not be able to do so. The patient would then feel all the more powerful and out of control. In the cases discussed in this chapter, the limits were set with the help of the parents, not unilaterally by the therapist. In outpatient treatment it is difficult to set limits without parental support and cooperation. The parents must be in accord with the action in order for there to *be* any effective action. If the parents have brought their daughter to psychotherapy willingly, because they feel that such treatment is necessary, their support can probably be elicited by the therapist pointing out the necessity for the action.

Dawn was another girl whose acting out needed to be stopped. Her troublesome behavior was of short duration, however; the attentions of a Childrens' Protective Service worker and a psychotherapist were used to stop it. Dawn was referred to psychotherapy by her social worker. She was fourteen years old and had been living in a foster home for the past year. She seemed to like the foster home well enough and she claimed to like her foster mother. For the past six weeks, however, she had been misbehaving. She lied to her foster mother several times, saying that she was going to babysit but spent the time with a boy from school instead. She had been missing from home several times and had been vague when asked where she had been. As a result, her foster mother was frequently angry with her. Once, when asked to bring the groceries into the house from the car, Dawn forgot the frozen foods and they were ruined. She seemed preoccupied when doing her chores and it took her hours to get her work done. This behavior picture was in total contrast to her former adjustment.

Previously, she had always been shy, pleasant, cooperative, and anxious to please. "What has happened to Dawn?" her foster mother asked.

In her sessions with the psychotherapist, Dawn was indeed pleasant, shy, and cooperative. She said she was upset but was having trouble figuring out why. She looked sad and perplexed. According to her history, she was the youngest of four children and the only girl. Her three brothers were placed in foster homes by the Childrens' Protective Service because their father beat them repeatedly. Dawn hardly knew her older two brothers, since they were placed when she was quite young. When she was twelve years old, her natural father started having sexual relations with her. She was frightened of him because he had beaten her brothers and her mother, so Dawn said nothing about it to her mother for a year. When her mother found out, she told the social worker. Dawn was placed out of the home, but no charges were brought against the father since no one could prove that he did indeed have sex with his daughter. Her mother always maintained that such actions on her husband's part were impossible and offered evidence to show that he could not have been with Dawn at the times she claimed he had. Nonetheless, Dawn was placed out of her home for her own protection.

Dawn saw her mother once a month and enjoyed her company, but she refused to go to the home because she was afraid to be near her father. For about two months prior to the beginning of Dawn's therapy, her mother had been making inquiries of the foster mother, wondering if it were possible for Dawn to return home to live with her. Dawn found out about this and told her mother that she would not come home until her father left the house.

In the meantime, Dawn was becoming unsure about her relationship with her foster mother. She wondered if she liked her. The woman did give her a birthday party, the first one Dawn ever had, but she invited several of her adult women friends to come over with their children; it did not seem that the party was really for Dawn. Also, her foster mother had recently opened a little gift shop and expected her three foster daughters to work there. Dawn spent all Saturday and Sunday in the store and did not have time to go skating. Besides, she had chores to do at home in addition to working in the store. All this seemed like a lot of work to Dawn; it did not seem fair. Yet her foster mother told her how much she liked her, and Dawn liked to hear this. Dawn was unsure whether her foster mother was using her or really liked her.

Dawn was still under pressure from her mother to return home, but she was frightened of her father. She was also beginning to wonder why she had to leave her home when her father was the one who had done something bad to her. Why was she being punished? Because of these thoughts, Dawn was upset, and her acting out was the result.

In the course of therapy, Dawn clarified her thoughts and feelings, which had previously been covered up by her acting out. She now understood what she wanted. She told her mother that she wanted to come home but that her father must be asked to leave first. She also told her mother that her marriage was not a good one; she worked to support her husband yet he beat or abused her children. The mother told Dawn that she had never thought about it that way before. Dawn's mother did think about it and eventually asked her husband to leave. Although she saw him occasionally, she did not allow him back into the home. She then asked Dawn to come home. Dawn was now ready to do so and gained her social worker's permission. Her therapy stopped with her return.

It is not easy for a fourteen-year-old girl to make judgments about the adults in her life, but Dawn had to do this. She needed the aid of her psychotherapist to help her understand what was happening and how she was feeling. While the limit setting was not as flamboyant as in some of the other cases, it was there nonetheless. If a mother, a foster mother, a social worker, and a psychotherapist all tell a fourteen-year-old girl that she must stop misbehaving and must instead think about what she is doing, she is likely to do exactly that; Dawn did. She stopped acting out long enough to figure out what she was reacting to and how she might accomplish her goals. The psychotherapist did not have an opportunity to witness the development of Dawn's identity, since the psychotherapy, which lasted for about seven months, terminated well before the end of Dawn's adolescence.

In the case of Linda, the benefits of limit setting are also demonstrated. Linda, fourteen years old, was brought to the psychotherapist by her parents because of her depression. She was tearful, irritable, and withdrawn. Linda's father worked as a counselor in a local junior college, and her mother taught in the same school. Linda had a sister one year younger than herself and a brother five years older. Her brother lived by himself most of the time, but he would occasionally come home to stay for a month or two; her sister had not yet started high school. Of the two girls, Linda was always considered by her parents to be the attractive and outgoing one. She resembled her mother and had always been close to her. Linda had many friends and her sister had none.

In her initial hours with the psychotherapist, Linda talked about her love affair with a handsome and popular boy, the president of the senior class. She had fallen in love and had her first sexual experience with him. Although she still loved him, he refused to see her anymore. Moreover, he had talked about their sexual escapade to other boys at school, much to Linda's embarrassment. Linda was now sexually active with many young men from her school, and her parents were aware of it. Linda shared her secrets with her mother; the two were uncommonly close. Linda's sexual activity took place without love and without a relationship. She was acting out her depression.

In a conference with Linda's parents, the problem of her sexual activity was discussed. The therapist tried to help Linda's parents see that their daughter's sexual activity and poor reputation were problems they must deal with. The parents were perplexed. It had been their philosophy that parents should not interfere with the sexual expression of their children. They felt that sex should be natural and that trying to inhibit it in teenage girls was hypocritical. Linda's parents were so certain of their philosophy that the therapist had difficulty convincing them otherwise. Eventually, the parents were persuaded that their daughter was too immature to handle sex and that she would not be ready until she was sixteen. The parents accepted this evaluation, and Linda's sexual acting out stopped. She continued with her psychotherapy for another eight months, and she was helped to understand the problems she had in relating to young men.

Linda was depressed following her experience with the first lover. She acted out her depression by floundering; she needed someone to show her what she must do. She had been an attractive, lovable, outgoing child who had suffered no real problems or frustrations in her life until the first lover stopped seeing her. She needed help handling her problems with boys, but the acting out had to end first. This was accomplished when her parents became convinced that limit setting was necessary.

Several years later, when Linda was twenty, she again saw the therapist because of a recurrence of her depression. The therapist was interested to learn that Linda had indeed had a two-year moratorium on sex between the ages of fourteen and sixteen and that she now felt better able to handle relationships with men. Linda was depressed because she could not decide on a career. She was in college, but she was finding the work difficult; she just could not make herself stick to her studies. She also described her life-style as a very dependent one. When not dependent on her parents—especially her mother—she would become very dependent on some young man. If he wanted to marry her, however, she became very upset. She did not realize that young men might interpret her desire for closeness as a desire for marriage; she only wanted someone to be dependent on. She seemed quite unaware of what she wanted.

As a result of her second course of psychotherapy, Linda learned to exercise greater control over her fears. Her self-confidence grew, and she was able to make decisions for herself. By the time therapy ended, she had found both an identity and a career. Seeing Linda in therapy six years later gave the psychotherapist an opportunity to see the effects of the limit setting on her acting out. Linda thought that the earlier advice of the psychotherapist was wise. She acknowledged that she had, indeed, been very depressed at the age of fourteen and acted out her depression. She had taken the therapist's advice because she recognized its value; she did not resent it.

Limit setting is necessary when the teenage girl takes on more than she can handle and becomes symptomatic as a result. Once she begins to act out, she is unlikely to stop unless there is external insistence that she do so—that is, unless some limits are set on her behavior.

FOUR

Depression in the Older Adolescent

Psychotherapy with the older adolescent girls is likely to be strikingly different from psychotherapy with a younger one. I usually use my few minutes of preparation time before one of the early sessions with a younger girl to summon the energy necessary to deal with the anticipated drives and undirected impulses of the thirteen- or fourteen-year-old. But if the next hour is to be spent with a sixteen- or seventeen-year-old, I use the time to clear my head for a more intellectual challenge. (Note that there is not a fixed age for the end of the earlier phase and the beginning of the later phase of adolescence; most often, the shift seems to occur between the ages of fifteen and sixteen.)

Depression, rather than acting out, is the most common presenting symptom of the older adolescent who comes to the attention of the psychotherapist. Certainly older girls act out, and treating these adolescents will be discussed in Chapter Five. However, the longer the acting out has been present, the more likely it is that a girl's parents have grown accustomed to the behavior and have come to expect it; they feel less urgency in seeking psychological help. Simply because she *is* older, the girl has probably been acting out quite a long time, and she may need to deal with her behavior on her own or with the help of friends — or even with the help of the juvenile justice system. This latter possibility alone reinforces the need to treat an adolescent's acting out as quickly as possible.

When she begins psychotherapy, the older adolescent knows that she is depressed and can, to some extent, talk about it. Although she is not sure *why* she is depressed, she is willing to discuss some of the things that bother her. She may say, for example, that her mother always does *this,* that father never does *that,* or that school pressures are a problem and the schools ought to change. She may complain that people are hypocritical, that the girls she knows are only interested in who has the newest clothes, or that these girls form their own little cliques and that she doesn't seem to fit into any of the cliques.

The depressed older girl generally develops a dependency on her therapist very rapidly and is readily influenced by her or him. When the parents support the psychotherapy emotionally or financially, the girl usually sees this as evidence of parental approval of such dependency and influence. The psychotherapy sessions provide support, attention, and an opportunity for the girl to vent her feelings about all the things that depress her. Within a few weeks, her depression lightens as a result. A calm, sympathetic, interested attitude on the part of the psychotherapist helps.

The underlying problems causing the girl's depression probably stem from the separation-individuation process, which occurs at about this age. The adolescent girl is trying to separate from her parents and become her own person who makes her own decisions and handles her own life. But this is a difficult and complex process and can — in a number of ways — lead to depression.

Masterson (1972), in his discussion of the borderline adolescent, mentions the adolescent's need to distance herself from her parents. He feels that a borderline adolescent, earlier, between the age of one year and three-and-a-half years, had great difficulty with the separation-individuation process, which occurs as a child attempts to break the symbiotic bond with her mother. A borderline adolescent developed intense abandonment fears at that earlier age, fears that she has never been able to work through. When a child with this borderline condition enters the teenage years and attempts to create some emotional distance from her parents, the earlier abandonment fear is revived and, according to Masterson, accounts for the anxiety, depression, and acting out seen in many adolescents. Blos (1967) also mentions that an adolescent needs to create some distance from her parents, but he feels that a second separation-individuation process actually occurs during preadolescence and adolescence, characterized by a psychic restructuring necessitated by the child's emotional disengagement from infantile objects. Anxiety, depression, and acting out can be generated in this second separation-individuation period. Although they may differ somewhat theoretically, both authors agree that an adolescent needs to emotionally move away from her parents and find her own identity.

Sometimes a girl spends less time with her family and confides in her parents less in an attempt to facilitate separation. One or two close friendships can help the adolescent girl immensely because she gains someone to confide in and become dependent on. Not being able to find a friend when she needs one can greatly contribute to her fear of separation from her parents; without friends or parents, a girl would really be on her own in the world. Without the social structure of the family, there might be no social structure at all for her; such a possibility would indeed be frightening.

On occasion, parents find the prospects of their daughter's separation distressing because of their own neurotic reasons. Parents can make a child feel guilty about, or incapable of, handling the world without their help to the extent that a girl's fear or guilt may increase if she makes moves to become more independent.

A girl's separation from her parents does not proceed according to any predetermined timetable but involves a series of actions and reactions. The girl makes a move and her parents react. The parent and the child are continually adjusting and readjusting to each other. For example, the daughter may wish to use the family car to go to the beach or to a friend's house in a neighboring city. She may be apprehensive about making such a trip for the first time, but she knows her friends can handle a drive to the beach and she wants to try. Although her mother is worried about her taking the car so far, she decides that it will be all right this time. The girl takes the car, reassured of her own capabilities by her mother's approval. All goes well. Several days later, the mother asks her daughter to go to the airport to pick up her grandmother. The mother is relieved not to have to make the trip herself, and the grandmother is impressed at how grown up her granddaughter is now that she drives so well. By this action and interaction process, the girl has gained a sense of mastery and a feeling of greater independence; she can do one more thing on her own.

Since the older adolescent has achieved greater separation from her parents than the younger adolescent, she will be more concerned about the difficulties she encounters in coping with the world. She will also be more concerned and fearful about her anticipated move away from home. Leaving home and coping with the difficulties of her current life are the two principal themes of psychotherapy with the older adolescent.

Therapy with the older girl is usually a more thoughtful and intellectual process than with the younger girl. The older adolescent will probably go into psychotherapy knowing how she feels, and she will be able to learn some of the dynamics that create these feelings in her. Not only does she seek explanations for her feelings, but she wants to learn how to change the depression or anxiety she experiences. She will be neither interested nor able to learn *all* about the psychodynamics that are occurring, but she wants to know something about why she feels so badly.

Libby, fifteen-and-a-half years old, sought psychotherapy because of a depression. A family situation contributed to the problems she was having separating from her parents. She expressed feelings of hopelessness and despair to her mother. She could hardly get herself to do her schoolwork or to spend time with her animals—which had previously been her "life." Although she had been slightly overweight as a latency-aged child and in her early adolescence, now she had lost her appetite and was losing weight. She skipped meals and then ate huge quantities of food, especially sweets, much to the consternation of her mother, who was concerned about this dietary imbalance. Her only sibling, a sister, was also concerned about Libby's eating habits, since Libby could "eat the kitchen bare," eating even those sweets her sister had baked for herself. At about this time, Libby's menstrual periods stopped, and then she started losing her hair. Libby became really worried and was eager for psychotherapy or whatever people felt would help her. She was glad to have lost weight but not her hair. Libby was carefully examined by her pediatrician and a gynecologist, both of whom referred her for psychotherapy.

Libby's parents had married young and poor, and both had struggled to "get ahead." Her mother had kept a series of increasingly larger homes running without help. She sewed for her daughters and did all of the gardening to save money. Her father worked long hours to make his business a success. The parents had few social outlets together. The mother had devoted her life to her daughters, particularly spending a great deal of time on their scouting activities, which required transportation to many events and competitions and many hours as a scout-parent leader. However, her husband, by now successful, wanted his wife to entertain more, travel with him more, and be glamorous like the wives of his business peers. Although she was quite aware of what her husband wanted, she refused to try to meet his expectations; she feared she was not sophisticated or educated enough to fit into that sort of social circle. She was self-conscious and hence angry with her husband for wanting her to do something she found frightening. She was also angry with him for having ignored her for so many years, and thus she refused to do what he wished.

Libby's mother had her daughters carefully tucked under her wing. But what about Libby, who wanted to venture out from under that wing? She could have rebelled, caused trouble, and gone her own way, but she really liked her mother and felt sorry for her. They had always been close, and her mother had always done so much for her; she felt disloyal whenever she thought of doing more on her own. Also, her mother's protective, ever-present aid may have contributed to Libby's uncertainty about handling things on her own. This was another reason why she did not rebel or separate more; instead she developed a clinical depression.

It is interesting that Libby was so distressed about being disloyal to her mother, for her younger sister did not appear to share this concern. Oldest children are often the most involved with their parents. Unlike their younger siblings, they do not have older children in the family to act as a buffer between them and their parents. Being the oldest may cause the child to achieve more, but by the same token the oldest has the greatest exposure to parental psychopathology (Goertzel and Goertzel, 1962; Monson and Gorman, 1976).

Libby's psychotherapy lasted about two-and-a-half years, ending when she left home to live with a friend. No medications were used, nor was she hospitalized. Her depression did not last the entire period she was in therapy, of course, but once the psychotherapy started Libby found that she needed support and guidance to deal with many situations even after she had achieved symptom relief. As her depression lightened, she became more difficult to live with, which in turn helped to effect some emotional separation from her mother. The mother did not like Libby's new behavior and complained of it to the therapist, but, interestingly enough, she did not forbid it, apparently feeling that it must be tolerated if Libby were to improve. Libby's mother's complaints about her daughter's irritating behavior were really complaints about her feelings of loss as her daughter became increasingly independent. To some extent, the mother came to realize this reason underlying her discontent.

The tone of the psychotherapy was one of dependence on the therapist and less dependency on her mother. Libby came to the sessions with complaints about her mother, father, sister, and peers. The therapist simply listened. After Libby tired of complaining about her peers, she asked advice and tried to improve her relations with them. After she tired of complaining about her parents, she began to separate slowly from her mother and then from her father—but not until she allowed herself to get to know him better. In her closeness to her mother, Libby had become alienated from her father and had avoided him; she needed to know him better before separating from him.

Children grow up identifying with each parent to some extent. After so many years of closeness to her mother, Libby had come to feel that there was nothing good about her father. Yet Libby found some personality traits in herself that she could also see in her father. Until she could at least partially accept her father, she could not accept those traits that they shared when she saw them in herself; she could not like herself. Only after she decided that her father was not all bad could she accept those personality characteristics they held in common, the result of her identification with him. If the therapist had not given her license to do so, it would have been extremely difficult for her to get to know her father better. Libby would probably have felt that she was being too disloyal to her mother.

It is clear that Libby's problems stemmed from her separation-individuation process. The mother's neurotic need for her accentuated Libby's difficulties. After becoming dependent on the psychotherapist, she also allowed herself to be influenced by the therapist; in turn, the therapist gave her both the license to separate and the emotional support she needed for such a maturational step.

The case of Kay is similar: she too was an older adolescent who became depressed, and she too had a lifelong history of being very involved with her mother. Kay was sixteen years old when she started therapy. She was referred by a gynecologist whom she had consulted because she feared she might be pregnant. Her first boyfriend (and first lover) had just left to join the navy. She was violently angry with the boyfriend for leaving her and became depressed and threatened suicide. How dare he do that to her! She was not noticeably upset about the possibility of being pregnant, just angry and depressed at his leaving. She wanted to kill herself, to kill him, or to sue him for everything he was worth—which, financially, wasn't much. She wanted revenge.

Kay's parents were not happily married. Her mother described herself as smoking too much and drinking too much; she complained of being lonely, of finding little companionship in her husband, who busied himself with his work and who was a very self-absorbed person. Kay was her mother's only and much-indulged child. Her mother stated that once, when Kay was five, she had spanked her; Kay had held her breath until she became red in the face, and her mother had never tried to spank her again. The mother also spoke of her own adolescent problems; she had been "too wild," staying out too late at night, drinking heavily and being promiscuous.

For the past several years, Kay had been modeling through an agency; actually she modeled quite often, with her mother as her ever-present companion and audience. Although Kay's depression looked serious during the first few office visits, it proved to be manageable through office psychotherapy alone; neither medication nor hospitalization was necessary. The mother was advised to be watchful and aware of what Kay was doing, to be sympathetic toward her, but not to be intrusive or to question her too much. Kay's mother followed this direct advice carefully.

Kay spent her first sessions venting her rage at her boyfriend for leaving her. After a while, though, she was able to talk about how difficult it was for her to separate from anyone significant in her life and how depressed she became whenever it seemed necessary to do so. She also talked about the death of her grandmother, which had been very difficult for her.

Interestingly, at the beginning of each session, Kay would ask the therapist how she was feeling before she would talk about her problems. If Kay could not get an answer, she would try to figure it out for herself. Only if she decided that the therapist was all right would she let her feelings of anger, rage, and depression erupt. Eventually, Kay was able to explain that she did not wish to burden the therapist or hurt her further if she were having a bad day.

In her relationship with the therapist, Kay behaved as she did with her mother. Kay and her mother were very considerate of each other—unusually so. This may be why Kay was so angry with her boyfriend. It had never occurred to her that, in a close relationship, people could ever do things to each other that might hurt. Her expectations of relationships, especially close ones, were unrealistic. Kay eventually came to that conclusion and started dating a young man with whom she developed a close relationship that was good, but not perfect. The couple became engaged, but Kay's mother insisted that the young man was not good enough for her daughter. The mother wanted her daughter to find a wealthy, attractive man from the international "jet set" who would be capable of giving her daughter everything and of making her forever happy. Although Kay's promising bank clerk did not meet these "qualifications," he was capable of giving Kay the attention she wanted and the limits on her behavior she needed.

Because of her closeness to her mother, Kay had difficulty separating and becoming her own person. She did not essentially change the nature of her dependency as a result of therapy, but instead transferred it from her mother to her new boyfriend. Importantly, and supported by the psychotherapist, she did not impulsively leap into a self-destructive relationship; she proceeded with caution to find someone who was comfortable with her dependency and who seemed more dependable than her first young man. Also, she came to see what one can reasonably expect in a close relationship, rather than continuing her unrealistic expectations, which were based on her close relationship with her mother.

Sheila's case is an example of an eldest daughter who worked so hard to fulfill her parents' expectations of her for leadership and scholarship that she did not take time to develop her own needs for friendships and closeness. Sheila was sixteen-and-a-half years old when her parents brought her to psychotherapy. She had developed crying spells and insomnia and sometimes could not make herself go to school. She complained of the burden of trying to do so much at school and of the pressure of doing so much at home. She did far more than her share of housework and cooking, since no one else in the family seemed to care if the house looked nice or if the family had meals together.

Sheila was the eldest of three children, with a sister two-and-a-half years and a brother four years younger. Sheila's sister was a good student, but not as good as Sheila. Her sister was always pressuring the parents for clothes, rides to friends' houses, and freedom to stay out late. In contrast, Sheila asked for little for herself and did a great deal about the house. She also assumed a position of leadership in many school activities, especially those that were intellectually oriented.

Sheila felt the pressure of all her self-assigned responsibilities and became increasingly irritable, tense, and depressed. For example, Sheila argued with students and teachers alike because nonbiodegradable products were used in the school cafeteria. Her tactics and irritability served to alienate her fellow students, and she lost her followers. She felt even more pressure to do it all alone. "How can I get anyone to care?" she asked. "No one cares!" "No one helps!" "Why should I have to do everything alone?"

In the course of her psychotherapy, Sheila became very dependent on her therapist and seemed to enjoy the fact that someone was looking after her. She became more relaxed and less depressed as a result of this attention.

Eventually, Sheila was encouraged to try to socialize more. She made the attempt, but it was ever so painful and without pleasure. She finally found a small group of girls to associate with, but she needed the approval of her therapist to spend time with them, since they were only good students—not the excellent ones she felt she should choose as friends. Yet, she found them so much less competitive and so much warmer than the girls she had tried to socialize with earlier. Her dependency on her therapist allowed her to compromise her standards, to modify her ego ideal.

In subsequent sessions, Sheila wanted to talk about what she might do to find friends when she went away to college. She wanted to prepare herself and talked about the problem at great length. By the time she did leave for college, she had several good ideas about how to develop new friendships. Sheila managed to cope in her new environment, but it was not easy for her. Both her fear of being away and her dependency on her therapist are apparent in the beginning of the first letter she sent to the therapist from college:

Dear Dr. L.,

It seems like years since I last saw you, even though it has been less than a month. I have managed to find some friends and have been fortunate in getting a friendly roommate. . . .

All three of the depressed, older adolescents described in this chapter developed some understanding of themselves and their problems because of their psychotherapy. Sheila learned that she needed to find friends in order to leave home comfortably and that she needed to compromise her values to some extent. Kay learned that close relationships are not perfect. Libby learned that she must find better ways to cope with the world so that her fears would lessen, and she learned that she was, in some ways, similar to her father, which was all right. None of the girls developed a great deal of insight, but they wanted to think things through a bit and find some explanations.

In all three cases, a therapist could undoubtedly find some psychopathology in the parents that contributed to the girls' depression. Indeed, a therapist might be tempted to deal with the girl's problem by recommending psychotherapy for the parents or the whole family. However, such a move hardly seems like the most effective way of helping the adolescent involved. Such a girl needs help immediately and cannot wait for her parents to change. Even if the parents *were* to change, the adolescent patient still has her own problems to deal with. She still has much to master, and much to decide, in order to feel self-confident and to increase her self-esteem. She must concern herself with her problems of leaving her family, of making friends, and of accomplishing her goals.

The priorities in working with adolescents are different from the priorities of doing psychotherapy with younger children. A child will most likely live with her parents for many more years, and the parents may need to change to facilitate their daughter's healthy development. The adolescent, however, has already come a long way; even though she has now come to an obstacle, she can hardly stop to wait for her family to change so that she can be freed of their problems and go about her task of separating. Even if she could wait, chances are that she would find it no less difficult to separate and to succeed on her own. She herself needs to develop more skills and more self-confidence — which can often be managed without the parents becoming involved in psychotherapy. Conferences with the girl's psychotherapist may be sufficient to help the family support the adolescent's changes.

Libby's mother, for example, had spent all her energies raising her daughters and participating in their activities, yet she did let her daughter leave. It was not easy for her to let go, she did complain to the psychotherapist a good deal, but she finally did allow her daughter to separate. Incidentally, two years later, the mother came to see the psychotherapist for a problem of her own, asking for support to leave her husband. Much to her satisfaction, she accomplished this goal. The mother's decision to come for psychotherapy also gave the therapist an opportunity to learn that Libby was still doing well.

In the case of Sheila, the girl with the enthusiastic and militantly high ideals, the parents recognized that they had contributed to her pressuring superego. They attempted to change their expectations of her, but it was too late; Sheila had incorporated their expectations as her own. It was her ego ideal that needed to change.

The term *ego ideal* is useful in understanding depression or dissatisfaction with one's self or with one's accomplishments. We all carry inside ourselves an ego ideal that determines the level at which we need to function in order to achieve self-approval and heighten our self-esteem. Our ego ideal might include some level of professional performance or of physical prowess or a personality trait that we feel we must reach or acquire and then maintain. If we cannot perform successfully in our profession or can no longer run the mile in eight minutes, or if we cannot remain pleasant and friendly but instead become bitchy and irritable, we may come to dislike ourselves or possibly end up being self-deprecating and depressed.

In the adolescent whose personality is less differentiated, the ego ideal can be changed by identification with an adult who is nurturing or caring and who thus assumes a parentlike role. The disturbed adolescent becomes so dependent on such an adult, frequently her therapist, that the relationship resembles that of a very young child with her parent. It is as if the adolescent has a second chance, a chance to relive an earlier formative period of life with a new parent who is more attuned to her psychological needs.

Teicher (1973) recalls that Lorand (1967) revived the concept of the ego ideal. Teicher concludes that "the root of the pathological depression is not being able to live up to the aspirations of the ego ideal" (p. 55). He feels that "the therapist is the transient ego ideal, and the newly acquired capacities for experiencing understanding, permissiveness, and love will be achieved through identification with the transient ego ideal" (p. 55).

The case of Thalia is an example of an older, depressed adolescent who learned to cope with her problems, one of which was her mother. Thalia, a sixteen-year-old black girl, was detained in one of the girls' units of a juvenile hall when the therapist first saw her. The unit supervisor had asked the therapist to see Thalia because the girl seemed depressed and uninvolved with the program in the juvenile hall; in fact, she seemed so disinterested that the supervisors found her difficult to relate to. In an interview, Thalia said that she was, indeed, depressed. The reason was, she felt, because she did not have access to street drugs. Thalia said that she normally used drugs to help her feel better. She liked amphetamines, LSD, and marijuana; they all made her feel good.

The therapist saw Thalia several times during her stay in the juvenile hall, and the girl became quite dependent on the therapist. Thalia related that she was the second of four children, all girls. She, her sisters, and her parents had lived together in a downtown ghetto area until two years ago. Her parents had decided to move to the suburbs so that the girls could attend better schools and have a better environment. The father had been in the military until his death in an automobile accident one year earlier. Thalia's older sister was using heroin, having started on the drug before the move to the suburbs; sometimes she stayed at home and sometimes with friends.

Since her husband's death, the mother had a great deal of difficulty handling the girls. She was, according to Thalia, overwhelmed by the responsibility of raising them. She tried to get her daughters involved with her church but was only successful in getting the youngest girl to attend. The mother became totally immersed in the church, and all her activities centered around it after her husband's death. She used guilt to try to control the behavior of her daughters, which Thalia resented. Although she did not respond to her mother's attempts to get her to behave differently, Thalia did respond to the guilt. The mother was perplexed

at Thalia's choice of friends from school — one Caucasian and one
Oriental. The three girls all wore patched jeans, hiking boots,
and backpacks, and all were using "street drugs."

Because of the therapist's attention and the group discussions in the juvenile hall, Thalia convinced herself that she must
stop using drugs and learn to handle the world without them. She
was released to a residential drug-treatment program, resolving
to "stay clean."

About a year later, Thalia's mother contacted the therapist,
asking if the girl could be seen in psychotherapy. Thalia was back
home again and, to her mother's knowledge, was not on drugs,
but she was depressed and not functioning well. Thalia had
graduated from the drug-abuse program; although she did not
want to live with her mother, she had no other place to go.
Appointments were set up to see Thalia once a week.

Thalia talked about her drug abuse in the past and her
determination not to return to that way of life. She said she had
become depressed again when she returned home to live. She also
talked about a young man she had met at the drug-treatment
program and thought that he might move to the area to be near
her. He was about to graduate from the program, was now
eighteen, and did not wish to return home to live with his parents.
Thalia feared it would be difficult for her mother to accept the
young man since he was Caucasian.

Thalia's young man did move to the area, and her mother
treated him coolly. Thalia was depressed because her mother did
not approve of him. She could see that her mother was trying to
make her feel guilty. By now, Thalia could readily recognize her
mother's maneuvers, but she still responded to them.

Eventually the therapist asked Thalia what she felt she could
do to get her mother to stop making her feel guilty. Thalia said
that she was sure that if she went to church her mother would approve of anything she might do: she might even approve of her
young man. The therapist convinced Thalia to go to church with
her mother regularly and to ask her boyfriend to go with them.
The three did go to church together almost every Sunday. Although Thalia and her boyfriend avoided the other church activ-

ities, her mother seemed satisfied. Thalia started feeling better, and she soon stopped her treatment. She was doing well and she had her man to confide in.

The therapist did not see Thalia again until she was nineteen. She had had a baby and was living with her boyfriend. All had gone well until quite recently, when her boyfriend started taking drugs again. She was unhappy and worried because she had strong urges to harm their baby. The therapist encouraged her to move back to be near her mother, who could help her with the baby. After a mourning period, when she grieved the loss of her man, Thalia seemed to again be adjusting well. She again terminated her treatment.

Thalia's case shows us an older adolescent girl who became depressed because she was unable to cope. Her psychotherapy was geared to helping her deal with her problems and develop a sense of mastery over them—one of which was her mother. When she learned to adjust to her mother more effectively, Thalia felt less depressed and less guilty. We can expect an older adolescent to learn to adjust to her parents as they are; her parents are part of her realities.

Beth is another example of a girl in the later phase of adolescence who became depressed enough to need psychotherapy. At sixteen, she was deeply troubled by both the prospect of leaving home and her fear that she could not meet her parents' expectations. She was the oldest of three daughters and had internalized her parents' values, especially her mother's values to achieve and to strive for perfection. Beth's mother was not willing to compromise her expectations of her daughter, but Beth had to learn to compromise her expectations of herself. She had to learn to achieve and succeed but not to expect perfection of herself in all areas. She had to learn to relate to people more comfortably so that she could prepare to leave home. She managed to do all this despite her mother's unwavering, unrealistic expectations.

Beth came to psychotherapy only after much urging from her parents; more reassurance was needed from the therapist. Beth's main concern was what effect being in psychotherapy would have on her "record," but at that time she was always concerned about her "record." Beth was attractive and intelligent and did very well in high school, receiving mostly "A" grades in advanced placement classes. She talked easily and seemed to possess social skills. She felt that her main difficulty in developing and maintaining friendships was not allowing herself to take the time to do things with her peers.

Beth complained of being extremely tired. She had crying spells and severe insomnia and was getting only about two hours of sleep a night. She also complained of depression and discouragement. She saw herself as unattractive, unintelligent, and lacking in talent, comparing herself to her younger sister whom she felt did even better in school than she and without trying as hard. (Her sister was a concert oboist as well as an outstanding student.) Beth also compared herself to a friend in school, a great achiever who always seemed to get a higher "A" than Beth on every paper and test, no matter how hard Beth tried. On the basis of these "comparisons," Beth had convinced herself that she was dull, uninteresting, and a mediocre student. Her view of herself compared to reality was an amazing distortion, yet she was quite serious about her feelings of unworthiness and was quite depressed.

In the first session, Beth immediately asked the therapist some test questions to determine whether or not the therapist approved of her parents. She asked if the therapist knew her parents. She wondered if the therapist had noticed how demanding her mother was. She tried to find out whether or not the therapist agreed with her father's political views. This was an interesting situation since Beth felt fairly free to criticize her parents, but if the therapist had joined her, there would have been no therapy. Beth sensed that basically she was not too different from her parents and that criticizing them was akin to criticizing herself. Besides, if the therapist had expressed negative views of her parents, Beth might have had to commit herself to opposing them if she did proceed with the therapy. She did not feel up to overtly opposing her mother; mother was a stronger personality than Beth.

When adolescents describe their parents, they really can make them sound bad. Many adolescents will attempt to convince their therapists that their parents are the problems; they are trying to deny their own problems by focusing on parental deficiencies. Joining the adolescent in such criticism reinforces her tendency to use denial.

In Beth's case, apparently the therapist acted wisely enough for the psychotherapy to continue. The first step was to allow a period of time for the dependency on the therapist to develop and the depression to lighten. Then the therapist emphasized to Beth the need for recreation, explaining that recreation meant to *re-create* one's energies. With such a rationalization, Beth could accept the need for some social and recreational activities. Beth began to plan each week with one scheduled extracurricular activity. She might play tennis or hike or go to a party. Her depression lightened even more. She had more energy and slept better. She continued to enjoy the attention the therapy situation afforded and, to please her therapist, scheduled even more time for social activities. Her school performance also improved, and she usually received the higher "A" in her competition with her friend.

Beth's mother continued her never-ending vigil to maintain the family's high intellectual values. One of her strategies was to select only very special television programs for her daughters and husband to view, and such programs could only be on the educational channel to qualify. Her expectations of her family's achievements never changed.

Beth spent the next summer on a kibbutz in Israel picking fruit; she returned thin and tanned and was happier and more relaxed than she had been for many months. Her mother was happy that Beth had lost weight. Actually, Beth was quite thin before she went to the kibbutz, but her mother felt that the thinner one is, the more one has achieved.

After high school, Beth went to an eastern college and did well there. During her sophomore year, she became engaged to a promising graduate student who came from the "right" kind of family, but her mother contacted the therapist in dismay because the young man was myopic. She found it hard to approve of him since myopia can be inherited and she wanted perfect grandchildren. It was apparent that the mother still had not changed, but Beth's ego ideal had changed to the extent necessary for Beth to be less depressed.

It is interesting that when she applied for college Beth asked if her therapist would be a reference for her. The therapist declined on the basis that their relationship had been a therapeutic one and that some admissions officers might not look on psychotherapy favorably. Beth accepted this explanation, but was still disappointed—the same young woman who was so concerned about her "records" earlier!

Beth is an example of an adolescent girl becoming dependent enough on her therapist to use the therapist as a transient ego ideal, which reduced her depression. As she became less depressed, Beth fairly easily learned to cope with her problems, including her mother. Her mother never changed; Beth adjusted to her.

The prospect of leaving home can precipitate depression in many older adolescents. Looking forward to graduation, planning for and selecting a college, getting ready to move out on one's own, or approaching one's eighteenth birthday (which the adolescent looked forward to so unambivalently three or four years earlier) can present a very stressful situation for the older girl. Many normal adolescents appear to anticipate leaving home and prepare for it by being away for finite periods of time prior to actually moving out, as if they wished to practice and gain confidence. Going to camp, taking a summer job away from home, traveling with a group, or visiting a relative in a distant city can help the adolescent gain confidence in her ability to cope outside the parental home by giving her some successful experiences and a sense of mastery. Some adolescents do not have this preparation, because either the preparation itself or the eventual goal is too threatening.

Tina graduated from high school with the intention of going to secretarial school, but she could not bring herself to actually enroll. She had never dreamed that this would be a problem: she was a good student and her parents were going to help her financially. But when it came time to start classes, she developed symptoms of depression.

After Tina had called to make the initial appointment, the therapist received this note from her mother:

March	Went to Dr. G. for Tina because the situation had become unbearable—she was tense, nervous, unable to sleep, and greatly depressed. He prescribed sleeping pills.
April	Situation not improved. Dr. G. referred us to Dr. B., a psychiatrist, who prescribed sleeping pills, Miltown, and first weekly, then monthly, visits. Eight visits into the summer. Outward symptoms appeared to improve.
July	Situation gradually worsened again and visits with Dr. B. resumed. Eight visits. All of us felt that Dr. B. wasn't getting to the heart of the matter. After consultation with him, visits were terminated in August. Spent some time deciding what the next step should be. Tina was calmer outwardly, was amicable, was helping with the household duties. Decision not to start classes in the fall had been decided earlier in the year.
October 8	Tina was severely depressed and had feelings of utter hopelessness. In the evening we could not reach Dr. B. After a long session with mother and father and Seconal, Tina was able to sleep. The next morning we had an emergency appointment with Dr. B. After three more visits, we felt sure he was not on the right track. He referred us elsewhere. He sent us to the university clinic. After lengthy discussion and research, the social worker referred us to you with the assurance that you would give this matter the urgency and serious attention it deserves.
October 24	The next days (Saturday and Sunday) Tina was very depressed most of the time. Tina will be eighteen next month; she has a brother fifteen years old. She graduated from high school last June and planned on starting business school in the fall, but that was changed to February because of her de-

> pression. Tina is creative and a perfectionist.
> Her really big interests are water skiing and
> music. She has always been an obedient
> child and an affectionate family member.
> She has introspected her problems to the ut-
> most. She and her parents need help.
>
> Desperately.

Tina had always been obedient and no problem to her parents until her recent depression. There was no real evidence of
adolescent rebellion and no evidence of separation from her parents; possibly there was no need for separation until she faced
the prospect of turning eighteen, going to business school, and
having a secretarial career that would eventually lead to leaving
home.

After the therapist saw Tina, the history was as predicted.
Tina's relationship with her parents had not been problematic on
either side. Only later did the therapist discover that the girl's real
anger was toward her mother, because she, the daughter, had to
start classes and prepare for her future while the mother could
stay home with her husband and her kitchen. This situation did
not seem at all fair to Tina. Prior to therapy, Tina had not found
the courage to rebel or to try to separate in any way. She had no
friends to lean on, and the family was a comfortable unit for all
its members; actually, until now, she had not needed outside
friendships.

In the course of the next eighteen months, as Tina proceeded with her psychotherapy, things became stormy at home.
Tina decided what the family was having for dinner, criticized
her mother frequently, and determined that her brother was
going to change his sloppy ways. Her mother and father became
obedient to her demands. Tina started in business school and
found two girls to car pool with. The next year she and a friend
found an apartment to share. But, before she left home, she demanded that she and her brother exchange rooms and that her
room be completely redecorated.

After eighteen months of the new Tina, her parents were
ready to see her leave home. Her rather demanding behavior

created distance between Tina and her parents. It also gave Tina a sense of strength and power, which made it easier for her to venture from the home.

Her mother had been right in her original note. The situation was urgent. Tina could easily have remained at home, perpetually close to her parents, and destined to a life of depression.

In Tina's case, we see an older adolescent who was having great difficulties with the separation process. She was so closely attached to her family and had developed so little separation that the rebellious tension she created between herself and her parents was an improvement over the previous, rather comfortable, dependency on her family.

Any psychotherapist who works with adolescent girls is likely to see many girls in the later phase of adolescence who have difficulty solidifying their identities or who are so dissatisfied with the identities they are developing that they are struggling to change them. Such adolescents will probably have depression as their presenting symptom. However, accompanying this depression can be a vagueness or a lack of definition. A girl may not have developed a clear-cut idea of who she is. She may feel that she does not fit into any of the cliques or subgroups at school, which happens when an adolescent does not have a fairly clear picture of her own identity.

Erikson (1959) writes that finding an identity is the main psychological task of adolescence. He describes *identity diffusion* as the state that develops when an identity cannot be found. He quotes Arthur Miller's character Biff in *The Death of a Salesman* as an example of identity diffusion. "I just can't take hold, Mom. I can't take hold of some kind of life."

Joanne was a sixteen-year-old girl with depression and an inability to find an identity when she sought psychotherapy — ostensibly because she thought she had a reading problem. She said she read slowly and felt so discouraged this past year in school that she had difficulty making herself finish her homework. Joanne, the second of three children, had a brother two years her junior and a sister four years older. Her sister was already in college, majoring in physics, and was described by Joanne as always sure of what she wanted and never deviating from her attempt to reach her goals. Her sister had had the same boyfriend since junior high school and seemed to feel no need to look for another. Joanne envied her sister's confidence in knowing what she wanted to do and who she was. Joanne complained of her own lack of direction and inability to feel comfortable with any of the groups of girls at school.

Very early in her psychotherapy, Joanne compared herself to her mother and talked of not wanting to be like her mother, but she feared that she might be. She stated that although her mother had a degree in engineering she had never used it; she stayed home to raise children and keep house. Yet her mother, as Joanne described her, was a terrible homemaker who cleaned the house only when guests were expected, which was rare, and who almost never cooked a dinner for the family. Joanne felt that her mother wasn't really a homemaker—*nor* an engineer. She knew her mother was a very nervous and upset person and described her mother's almost daily screaming spells. Although she described her mother's problematic behavior, Joanne was always careful not to criticize her mother when talking to the therapist. Instead, she would explain the pressures her mother was under or would blame herself, saying that the children probably made her mother nervous and that she, Joanne, was the one who seemed to irritate her the most. The therapist felt that Joanne needed to minimize her mother's misbehavior in order to avoid recognizing the intensity of her anger toward her. If she recognized it, she might go home and criticize her mother more. Joanne seemed to sense that such an action would profit her little.

Joanne's "reading problem" seemed to disappear after one or two psychotherapy sessions, and she spent the next two years working on her identity. She didn't want to be "super straight" like her mother who never drank, who never smoked, and who never had kissed a man until she was engaged to her would-be husband. But, Joanne didn't want to be part of the drug-abusing scene either, for she considered drug abusers as having given up on life. She thought she wanted to be an achieving person, a person who attained some prestige, but she also wanted to be feminine.

Joanne learned to sew but did not know what type of clothes

she wanted to make. Eventually, she started to make what she called "freaky clothes for freaky people" and located a market for them in a boutique. The next summer, Joanne went to work in one of the national parks as a waitress. She enjoyed the experience and the young people she met; she found that she could tolerate being away from her mother, be happier, and be successful in making new friends. She continued to improve in her dress designing and readily sold the clothes she made. Later, she and another young woman opened a boutique of their own.

Joanne had found an identity for herself; she considered herself an achiever but also a feminine and artistic person. Moreover, in contrast to her mother, her talents were practical ones, and she put them to good use. Joanne required a great deal of support from her therapist to try different things to see what she could do and what she wanted to do; it was essential for the therapist to be patient and encouraging throughout this process.

Not all depressions in the adolescent are of the neurotic or reactive type. Particularly in later adolescence, but actually at any time, manic-depressive illness can present itself. The adolescent with a manic-depressive illness can go to a hospital's emergency room or to a psychotherapist's office with many of the same presenting complaints as the neurotic adolescents discussed in this chapter. She may go to a therapy session depressed, complaining about her parents being too restrictive or not meeting her needs. She may be critical of the school system or the world. She may rebel against authority and complain that teachers are against real education or that her parents are too materialistic — as do so many adolescent patients and nonpatients alike. At the onset, the manic-depressive adolescent may sound the same as the neurotically depressed adolescent. Undoubtedly there are problematic situations in the family or the school that could be viewed as precipitating factors for the depression.

Recognizing that an adolescent is suffering from a manic-depressive illness is a complicated process. When they bring their daughter to the psychotherapist for her depression, the parents may be hesitant to relate the family history of this hereditary problem. It is not hard to understand the reluctance of these families to compare their daughters' problem to other tragedies in the family, but their reluctance can delay the course of effective treatment.

Joyce was brought to a hospital emergency room after her parents found her intoxicated at home, saying that she wished to die and telling her parents of her thoughts to kill herself by drinking chemicals used in their swimming pool. A week earlier, her parents had found Joyce in her room trying to hang herself. She had been drinking at that time, too. A sixteen-year-old in high school, Joyce was studying for final exams. She had always done well in school, but it had been an effort for her to do so. Joyce's one sister was away at college and could not give her the help with her studies that she had done in the past. Joyce's only brother was just a year younger than she and an excellent student who did better academically and socially. Joyce had always become depressed when exams approached, but it was worse this time, and the family felt that it could have been because the sister was away and unable to help her.

After a short hospital stay, with only a little medication for symptomatic relief, some arrangements were made for Joyce to finish her schoolwork by completing only the minimal requirements. Joyce appeared improved and went home but continued with office psychotherapy. She seemed to be doing well, and after graduation she went away to an art school that was considered less pressuring than a regular academic college. This school was also close enough to home so that Joyce could see her parents and her therapist as needed.

Near the end of the first year of art school, Joyce again became upset, but this time she was "high." When seen by the psychiatrist again, she was thinner, exuberant, showed a flight of ideas and pressured speech. She pleaded with the psychiatrist not to stop her from being "high" because it felt so good. She had been able to talk with boys for the first time and, in fact, had been awake for three days and nights, spending much of this time in conversations with various young men from school. In her dormitory, she played her radio loudly and then defied the rules. The students she roomed with had at first found her changed behavior humorous but soon became quite irritated with her.

Joyce was hospitalized again and, after a brief stay, calmed down and was able to return to school, but now as a commuting student, living at home. At this time, Joyce's parents revealed the family history of manic-depressive illness. The grandfather was in a nursing home with the family illness and not with senility as previously reported.

Even though Joyce's illness was not recognized at the outset, the treatment might not have been very different in the early stages. The psychotherapy Joyce received was directed toward helping her to get back into school and helping her to learn to relate better to her peers and improve her general problem-solving ability. Since psychotherapy has been shown to be useful with schizophrenics in conjunction with the medication they receive (Lamb, 1976; Hogarty and others, 1974, pp. 615-616), it is possible that medication and psychotherapy might also be helpful with manic-depressive patients. Some biologically oriented psychiatrists would take exception to this view. Hudgens (1974) described his study of two groups of adolescents, one group hospitalized for psychiatric problems and the comparison group for medical or surgical problems. He found an equally large number of adolescents in each group whom he considered to be suffering from manic-depressive illness. As treatment, he recommended the use of tricyclic, antidepressive medication, and lithium without suggesting psychotherapy. It seems to me that Hudgens must have been somewhat overenthusiastic in his search for this illness to find it so frequently in his comparison group, and I disagree with his deemphasis of psychotherapy. While I do not suggest that we should be too eager to "discover" manic-depressive illness in adolescent patients, it is important to remember that this illness can present itself in adolescence.

The older adolescent who comes to psychotherapy is more likely to ask for help for herself than the younger girl, for she is usually more aware of her feelings. The older girl who comes for therapy is often depressed; many of her problems stem from the separation-individuation process that occurs at about this time in her life. She is separating from her parents and becoming an individual with her own identity. The older girl becomes dependent on her psychotherapist, as does the younger adolescent, but the psychotherapist will usually be able to deal with her directly.

There will be less need for parent conferences and environmental manipulation since she is usually ready to learn to cope with her problems herself. As she does, she will develop more self-confidence and become less depressed. Psychotherapy with the older adolescent is also a more intellectual process. This older girl is able to understand some of the reasons for her depression and can come to understand some of the dynamics that caused it.

The degree of psychological sophistication and the maturity of the adolescent must be kept in mind when doing psychotherapy with her. A rational and supportive approach will be most effective in helping the older adolescent girl arrive at needed insights, learn to cope with the demands and expectations she faces in the world, learn to adjust her expectations of herself to appropriate goals, and overcome her depression.

FIVE

Acting Out in the Older Adolescent

Jackie, who is almost seventeen, has been caught shoplifting. She tried to take a pair of jeans and a sweater from a department store. She has been coming home late every night and sometimes does not get home until the next afternoon. She spends each evening with a different young man. She has not been going to school. What can be done to help her? How can psychotherapy be of help?

The type of limit setting that was so helpful with the younger girl—the strong, unambivalent stand against the behavior—will probably not be as effective with the older adolescent. The acting out of the younger girl was so impulsive, so out of control, and so provocative that she invited strict, definite limits on her behavior.

99

Her response to these limits was either to accept them blindly or to fight them without too much thought, and then to capitulate.

The older adolescent requires more of an explanation from the adults who are trying to curtail her acting out. She needs to be told why she must stop the behavior or in what ways the behavior is harmful or destructive to her. For example, if the parents do not feel it is wise for their younger adolescent daughter to go someplace, they can simply say, "No! You may not go there." The young adolescent's response may be to pout or to have a tantrum, but she will probably not go. Without more of an explanation, the older adolescent will not likely heed the objection of her parents. The parents will need to convince her with some sound reasons, such as saying, "We don't want you to go there. It's dangerous! Three boys were in a fight there last night. One ended up in the hospital. If you're planning to use our car, you and Jill will just have to go somewhere else!"

The older adolescent has usually separated more from her parents than has the younger girl. She has developed more skills and has made more decisions on her own, and thus she is in a better position to question authority. She is less fearful of her parents withdrawing their love and protection. She may feel that she could survive without them or at least without their emotional support. Without an explanation, limits are not likely to be effective; the girl may not follow the restrictions unless she is told why they are necessary. Setting limits with an older adolescent girl must be a more thoughtful process.

A psychotherapist can be helpful to an older adolescent by helping her see the consequences of her behavior, by helping her see what she may suffer or lose as a result. The older adolescent may not trust her parents' judgment in such matters. Many adolescents have learned that their parents' prohibitions on their actions are not always thoughtful, parental concerns but sometimes selfish, emotional responses. A psychotherapist can help the girl by showing her how she behaves, why, and the price she is paying for the behavior. If the older adolescent is convinced that altering the behavior is in her own best interests, she will probably discontinue the behavior or let her parents stop her. She has greater restraint than the out-of-control, impulsive younger adolescent.

With the older adolescent, acting out may be a sudden, un-expected episode of disruptive behavior that is a call for help; it may be symptomatic of some underlying problem. But there is another possible reason for acting out. One must remember that the older adolescent has a clearer idea of what kind of person she is; her identity will be more formed than that of the younger girl. If her acting out has been going on for some time, she may think of herself as delinquent; this conception then becomes part of her identity. Her actions in defiance of the ethics of her family or the laws of her community may be consistent with her delinquent self-identity. The psychotherapist working with an older adolescent must determine something about her identity before trying to help her understand her behavior or conflicts.

Consider, for example, the case of Jackie mentioned earlier. Her identity must be determined prior to trying to help her. The psychotherapeutic approach will be different depending on whether or not she has a delinquent identity. If Jackie has been delinquent for some time and has broken the law many times before, and if this is, in fact, the fourth time she has been arrested for shoplifting, neither her neighbors, her parents, nor Jackie herself will be surprised by her actions. She herself expected it; this behavior is part of her identity. If, however, Jackie has never really misbehaved before the last couple of weeks, and was, in fact, a good student and previously shy and fearful of boys, everyone—including herself—will be surprised by the behavior. Her actions are "out of character." It is likely that her acting out is a plea for help.

If Jackie's shoplifting and generally irresponsible attitude are not her identity, the psychotherapist can immediately try to respond to the call for help by trying to find out what problem or conflict is causing the sudden change in her behavior. If Jackie feels that her plea for help is being heard, she probably will be persuaded fairly easily to stop the behavior. Perhaps Jackie was subjected to some recent stress and felt she could not directly ask for help. For example, it could be discovered that while the mother was out of town visiting her ill grandmother Jackie's step-father of seven months tried to rape her. When her mother returned, still upset over the grandmother's illness, she became angry with Jackie for being cold and irritable with her new step-father. She accused Jackie of trying to make her life more miser-able and of being jealous of her attentions to her new husband. Jackie's frustration and anger may have precipitated her outburst of acting out. If Jackie, or another older adolescent girl with a sudden episode of disruptive behavior, becomes involved in psy-chotherapy, she will probably stop the behavior; the plea for help has been answered.

In contrast, let us think about the history a therapist might obtain if Jackie were more delinquent. Her staying out late, shop-lifting, and promiscuity might be chronic problems. Her behavior toward her mother might be characterized by open defiance and hostility. In her anger and in retaliation for the wrongs she feels she suffered because of her mother, Jackie might even have tried to seduce her new stepfather while her mother was away; such a feat, if she could have accomplished it, would surely have put the mother in an awkward situation which Jackie could then enjoy. If Jackie has been delinquent in this manner for some time, the psy-chotherapist will need to show her that her behavior is self-destructive or of little use to her before she will attempt to control it. Jackie must understand not only the meaning of the behavior but the price she is paying for it. For example, Jackie can be helped to see that the juvenile court was serious when it warned her that she would be placed out of her home if she were appre-hended again. She could be told that being in a foster home or in an institution is not as exciting as she may think. She would not have a room of her own. She would not be able to shop—let alone shoplift—if she were placed in a closed institution, such as a con-vent, because she would have no freedom at all. Perhaps she could be asked what she feels she needs to do to get along with her mother; does her mother really expect her to behave like an angel or just to "cool" her open defiance of everything and everyone? Or Jackie could be asked what she thinks will happen if she manages to seduce her new stepfather; will he leave or will her mother send her away? If Jackie can be convinced to change her behavior, or at least to modify it, she has enough self-control to do so. The psy-chotherapist will still have much to do, of course. Jackie still needs attention from someone who cares what happens to her, and she still needs advice and guidance from that person, but Jackie *can* modify her behavior.

The approach to psychotherapy with the older adolescent girl who acts out is dictated by the girl's identity. Regardless of her identity, however, the psychotherapist and her parents will need both to limit her behavior and to explain to her *why* she must stop it. With an explanation and a deterrent, she can stop herself; her behavior is under her control.

Another example of the need to assess a girl's identity before trying to help her can be found in the following incident. A psychiatrist and a medical student talked with an older adolescent girl who visited a drop-in clinic. The girl told them a long and vague story about why she was there, what she needed, and why her mother must not be contacted. She talked very slowly and with pauses, and the story changed several times in the telling. She appeared to be quite comfortable in the clinic and clearly did not wish to leave, yet she seemed to have little of substance to discuss with the psychiatrist. The psychiatrist told her that she could sit in the waiting room and look at the magazines for a while, and, if necessary, she could ask to be seen again.

The student, when alone with the psychiatrist, said that he felt they had overlooked something by not talking with the girl longer. Both agreed that she seemed to be manipulative and lying. The student, however, insisted that a person does not lie unless he is frightened, and the student wanted to find out what this girl was so frightened about. In reply, the psychiatrist said, "Perhaps you do not lie unless you are frightened, but there are some people who do lie even when they are not frightened." The student argued, insisting that his mentor must be wrong; he seemed to feel the psychiatrist lacked empathy and concern.

The medical student was not yet prepared to deal with the delinquent adolescent. He had not learned to consider the differing identities people develop. The psychiatrist felt that the girl was under the influence of some drug and that she felt more comfortable with people than alone. She stayed in the waiting room for about a half hour and then left. She was near people and this was probably what she wanted. If he had been alone in this situation, the student—like many novices in the mental health field—

might have expended considerable energy to "determine the cause" of the girl's anxiety and to try to "help" her. Occasionally such a naive and enthusiastic newcomer is able to effect some changes in his charge, simply because of his or her determination and optimism. Most often, however, the final result is some resentment on the part of the would-be helper who feels "used."

In the case of Melissa, an outburst of acting-out behavior was clearly a cry for help. Neither her therapist nor her mother needed to monitor Melissa's behavior; she did that herself when motivated by her mother's disapproval. Melissa, a sixteen-and-a-half-year-old junior in high school and an only child, was brought in by her mother for an evaluation. The mother's tone of voice when asking for the appointment and in the first evaluation hour was one of quiet desperation. She had come home from work a little early one day and found Melissa in her bedroom, naked, high on marijuana, and with a young man. The mother was horrified; she had never expected this of Melissa. Melissa had never dated and had not talked of any boyfriend, and the scene took her mother by surprise. She was so shocked that she could not discuss it with Melissa, but she did ask her daughter if she wanted some counseling. The mother made an appointment and told Melissa when it was to be—two days after the bedroom scene.

Melissa and her mother came together for the first appointment and talked to each other in the therapist's office about what had happened. The mother asked Melissa how long she had known this boy. Melissa said she had seen him at school for the past year; they had never talked, but she knew who he was. About two weeks earlier, he had come over to her house after school. They had smoked some marijuana and had sex—the first time Melissa had tried either. He had come over many times in the past two weeks for repeat performances. Since he did not have a car, a friend would drive him over and wait outside or return to pick him up just before the mother was due home from work. Since that first afternoon, Melissa and the boy had talked briefly at school a few times, but they had not gone out on any dates or seen each other except when he came to "visit."

Melissa's mother explained that she was not terribly shocked at a girl Melissa's age having sex, but she was upset since she did not feel that there was any relationship between the two and that the boy was taking advantage of Melissa. She explained that Melissa was very shy and had difficulty relating to anyone and especially to boys her own age. How could her first social contact with a young man lead immediately to a sexual encounter?

Melissa said that she did not feel that Ted was taking advantage of her. She was old enough to know what she was doing. She wanted him for a boyfriend, and she knew that he would not continue to see her if she did not have sex with him. She cried and was embarrassed as she talked about Ted. Although she put up some protest to her mother's urging her to stop seeing him, it was clear that she would do what her mother wished; she was much too embarrassed to do otherwise.

Melissa's mother was a single parent. She and Melissa's father had divorced many years ago, and he lived out of state. Her mother denied that there were any bad feelings between her and her husband at the time of the divorce but said that the marriage simply had been a mistake; they were too young. Melissa's father had remarried, yet he still sent money to help with Melissa's support. He had no other contact with either Melissa or her mother. Melissa was surprised to hear that her father contributed to her support; she had not seen him in years, and she and her mother never talked about him. In fact, they seemed to discuss very little. The mother said that she was not the sort of person to sit down and talk things over but that she should have talked more to Melissa about many things over the years. At the end of the first hour, Melissa agreed to come in for weekly appointments.

In her therapy sessions, Melissa admitted to leading a rather lonely life. As an only child, she had become accustomed to being alone after school. Although she had two girlfriends whom she saw occasionally, one lived rather far away (Melissa did not yet have a driver's license) and the other had a boyfriend whom she was spending a lot of time with. Melissa complained that her mother had a very demanding job as an office manager for a large company with a great deal of responsibility. She would come home tired at night and get angry if Melissa had not started dinner. Melissa also said that her mother sometimes went out for a drink after work with people from the office and came home late, but of course, she always called to tell Melissa when she would be late. Most of her mother's friends were single, and her social life did not include Melissa. The two of them went to her grandmother's place for holidays and saw their relatives, but there were not very many of them—only the grandmother, a teenage male cousin, and his father.

Melissa seemed to have few social skills and little experience in socializing. Her life was a lonely one, as apparently was her mother's. Her mother described herself as the wrong person to help Melissa gain social skills since she herself was not social or outgoing.

Melissa used her first few hours in therapy to cry and mourn the loss of her boyfriend. She has asked him to continue seeing her even though she could not have sex with him at the present time. He refused, saying that he must have sex if he were going to see her.

After a period of mourning her loss, Melissa was encouraged by her therapist to involve herself in some activities at school and in the community—to practice her driving and get her driver's license, to see her two girlfriends and invite them over to her house, to find a part-time job where other young people were hired. At first Melissa was overwhelmed by the therapist's suggestions. She did agree to get her driver's license. Eventually she joined a social group at school and enjoyed it, even though it made her somewhat anxious to be in that kind of situation. She resisted finding a job, but she did obtain volunteer work at an organization that needed many young helpers, both male and female. This volunteer work also frightened her, but she was able to do it. She was learning social skills and reported that she was happier than she had been in years. Her psychotherapy, which lasted about six months, enabled her to get out into the world and master her fears by learning social skills. She wanted no other help.

In Melissa's case, a lonely, isolated girl who lacked social skills had an affair, which was her way of acting out. This was not like her usual behavior; it was out of character. The affair did, however, allow her to relate to a young man and try sex. Though she lacked social skills, her relationship with Ted required none.

Because of her outburst of acting out, Melissa received the help and attention she needed. Neither her mother nor the therapist had to try to control Melissa's behavior. She controlled the behavior herself, motivated by her embarrassment and her mother's wishes.

An outburst of acting out also brought Roberta to psychotherapy for a brief period. Roberta, sixteen years old, was referred for an evaluation by her probation officer and the juvenile court. Roberta had been dragged, kicking and screaming and fighting, from a class in school. She attended a special, half-day school for unmotivated students who had not yet reached the age when they could legally discontinue their education. She had started a fight with another girl who had asked her for a "drag" off her cigarette just before class was to begin. Roberta, high on some street drug, took the girl's demand as a challenge and the fight ensued. Roberta was a good fighter, and it took several police officers and school officials to subdue her and take her to the juvenile hall. The next day, Roberta complained about the way she had been handled but was calm and cooperative, and she was released on condition she go for a psychiatric evaluation.

Roberta was the fourth of five children. The boys in the family had had brief escapades with the police, but there was no serious delinquency. Her older sister was in the Navy, and only Roberta and her brother, one year younger, lived at home. Roberta's mother was employed as a secretary and was a passive, compliant woman who allowed her husband to make all the decisions. The father was a truck driver who frequently fought with men at work and often beat his wife and children. Roberta had had many physical fights with her father, as had her older brothers. It wasn't just a matter of her father spanking or beating her; she fought back. Under her father's tutelage, Roberta learned how to fight quite well, as the school staff had occasion to see. Although Roberta had never engaged in any significant delinquent behavior, she had been in one fight in the regular high school she was attending two years earlier and had been expelled.

Roberta was amazed when, at the end of the evaluative session, the therapist recommended that she return for weekly psychotherapy. She took this as an accusation; she felt the therapist

was saying she was "crazy." Her mother's reaction to the recommendation was also one of surprise—that this was rather harsh
discipline for one fight at school. But after thinking about it for a
week or so, the family agreed that Roberta should see the therapist for six months.

After she started her weekly sessions, Roberta did not know
how to use the time. She asked repeatedly what she was supposed
to do now that she was in therapy. Eventually, she started talking
about her interest in animals. She could trust animals; even mean
and difficult animals were easier for her to trust than people. She
stated that she wished all people, including herself, would die and
leave the earth to the animals. She did not like her school and
wanted to return to a regular high school. She had figured out a
way to attend a high school out of her district by using her aunt's
address, but she seemed to want the support of the therapist to do
so. She probably wondered if she would be able to handle a regular school with its greater academic expectations.

Roberta transferred schools by using her aunt's address—
although the aunt lived close by, she was in another county.
Roberta appeared satisfied with her new high school. She did not
know anyone there, which was to her liking. The therapist was
concerned that because of the way she dressed Roberta would invite criticism from the other students. So the therapist told
Roberta that her black bra and her red plaid bra, worn under her
see-through blouses, with her dirty jeans and her dirty cowboy
boots, would cause the other students to comment about her
clothes sooner or later. She was told that these clothes made her
look "hard" and not very feminine. Roberta's reaction to this was
strong: "Whatever gave you the idea that I *wanted* to look feminine?" The therapist told her that it seemed that she *did* wish to
look feminine but that she was not successful in accomplishing it.
"That's the dumbest thing I ever heard," Roberta shouted as she
left the session early.

Roberta returned for the next week's session dressed in clean
jeans, sandals, and a black T-shirt with an obscene phrase sequined on the front. She asked the therapist in a provocative
manner if that was what she wanted her to wear. The therapist
said that she had not exactly gotten the idea—that the clean jeans

were an improvement, the sandals much better than those old cowboy boots, and certainly no one could see through that T-shirt, but that Roberta must not quite understand the idea of feminine. She asked if the girl didn't have another top without any sequined phrases. This time Roberta was more puzzled than angry. She really was not sure what the therapist meant by dressing in a feminine manner. But, she was also puzzled about why she was trying so hard to do what the therapist suggested.

Gradually, Roberta dressed in a much less abrasive manner, though still casually. As her dress changed, so did other aspects of her behavior. She became easier to talk to and less angry in her attitude. She talked about her fear of men. She feared that if she let herself get involved with any male she would be hurt, and she was not about to let anyone hurt her. She admitted that she sometimes fantasized about finding the perfect man. He would be very kind and true to her, and he would love animals as she did. Perhaps he would just ride up someday on his horse.

Roberta's therapy lasted exactly six months, as had been agreed. At the time of termination, Roberta was reminded that she could come back to see the therapist anytime she wanted. She was calmer, doing fairly well in school, going to occasional parties where she met young men without getting into any fights. She hoped to eventually find a job as a veterinarian's assistant.

Roberta's fight, her outburst of acting out, was, indeed, a plea for help. To protect herself against being hurt by anyone, she had developed an abrasive, hard exterior and manner, but her defensiveness was isolating her. She wanted help to get out of the lonely place she found herself in. She accomplished her goal. Her psychotherapy was brief but directed to her underlying problem. The acting-out behavior was rarely mentioned. She was an adolescent who wished to change her identity, or at least to modify her identity, and who was able to do this with the aid of her psychotherapy.

Nancy's case describes some of the techniques of dealing with a girl who had developed a delinquent identity and also demonstrates the more intellectual or logical approach to dealing with the acting out of the older adolescent. Nancy, sixteen years old and the youngest of four children, was referred for psychotherapy by a probation officer and her family doctor. She had left home five weeks earlier with her twenty-year-old boyfriend; they had just been located by the police because they could not pay their motel bill. This was the third time Nancy had run away from home with her boyfriend, but never for this long a period.

Nancy's history described a grade-school child who was "perfect" — she did well in her classes, was pleasant, and related well to adults. She was her father's pride and joy. After the eighth grade, Nancy was sent to a private girls' boarding school, the same one that her older sister had attended. Her two older brothers had attended local parochial high schools. The eldest boy had been in some trouble because of his acting-out behavior as an adolescent; he now lived alone, still supported by his parents, was unemployed, and led an isolated life. Her other brother and sister were attending college and apparently were adjusting well.

In her first year at boarding school, Nancy got into trouble with the school authorities for drinking in the dormitory and for not studying. She was asked to leave before the term ended. The next year she attended a local private school as a day student and again did poorly. She did not finish the first term since she was again asked to leave because of her drinking, her flagrantly hostile attitude, and her disruptive behavior.

Nancy's acting out had gone on since the beginning of high school. Although her parents did not like their daughter's continued acting out, they never had made any definitive moves to stop it. They rescued her, helped her out of trouble, and moved her to another setting when her acting out became intolerable to school authorities. Nancy's therapist got the distinct impression that her parents felt their role was to cover up Nancy's behavior when it became acute. They seemed to assume that her acting out was inevitable. Besides, they were so interested in their own activities, in their own travel and social lives, that they had failed to exercise any sustained effort to help their daughter change.

Nancy's acting out was, by now, part of her. Her parents expected it, and so did she. She saw herself as one who does not succeed but who disappoints herself and her parents; this was part of her identity. She had almost no friends and was lonely and hungry for a sustained relationship. She met her young man in a local hangout frequented by drug-using and drinking youth who seemed to be going nowhere. John was probably hungry for a relationship as well. He was extremely possessive of Nancy and wanted to be with her all the time. He was jealous if she confided in any female acquaintances or saw anyone else; he was also jealous if she spent time with her family, and, as often as he could, he interfered with her relating to them.

Nancy's parents probably would have tolerated Nancy's interest in John if the young man had visited with them and tried to fit in with the family instead of encouraging Nancy to run away. Because they were concerned about "appearances," they did not want Nancy to behave in ways that would raise the eyebrows of their friends and neighbors. Her parents urged Nancy to quit seeing John; then they became determined to stop the relationship and brought her to psychotherapy. Their determination impressed Nancy. She tentatively thought of doing what they wished, but she also wanted the companionship and intimacy with John desperately. She knew she would be very lonely without him.

Nancy and John began to have misunderstandings. Several times when he called she was in a bad mood, either because she had just come from the therapist or had been drinking. Her rudeness to him over the phone angered John, and he did not call for several days. Now it was Nancy's turn to become indignant, for John started seeing another girl from the hangout. She became very upset and refused to see John for a week or so.

With the help of her psychotherapist, Nancy came to see that John was selfishly possessive of her and that he wanted a woman he could possess because of his insecurities. If she were to be that woman, she could neither develop herself nor be a part of her family again. She started to think about what she wanted for herself. John eventually lost interest in her and found another girl. Nancy won him back just long enough for her to tell him to leave forever. She stopped seeing John for her own, not her parents' reasons. When she decided she wanted to do so, she was able to end the relationship.

After she stopped seeing John, Nancy stayed home a lot more

and tried to be close to her mother, but she rediscovered that her mother did not have time for such closeness. Nancy again started drinking and missing school; her acting out returned for a short time. She had tried to be the perfect angel she had once been but felt it did not suit her. Her parents did not want to spend much time with their daughter, even if she did act like a perfect little angel. Therapy helped Nancy to see that she needed to make some plans for her future. She decided she wanted to improve herself and planned to become a secretary. She took typing in school, and she found a part-time job to help her become independent.

Nancy terminated her psychotherapy when she was eighteen years old. She knew her therapist would be moving from the area in a few months and was annoyed at her dependency on the therapeutic relationship. She terminated rather than allowing the therapist to leave her, much like her method of ending her relationship with John. She had won him back just so she could break off with him rather than letting John leave her—she quit so she could not be fired. Before termination, however, she spoke of further psychotherapy in the future and asked for a referral.

Nancy's acting out was part of her, part of her identity. Although her parents disliked the behavior, they tolerated it and rescued her time and again. Originally, her acting out may have been an indication that she was not mature enough to live away from home. But the pattern of her parents' rescuing her, instead of stopping her, allowed the behavior to continue long enough to become part of Nancy's identity. Through therapy, Nancy's behavior was modified to the point where it was less self-destructive, but this could only be accomplished by convincing her that she needed to modify the behavior herself. She learned how it was in her best interests to change, and then she did so.

I am not suggesting that the treatment of an older acting-out adolescent is entirely an intellectual process and that a psychotherapist can, through logical argument, dissuade her from acting out. In this case, for example, Nancy's parents were adamant that she should no longer see John. Many family arguments occurred during the course of psychotherapy. Although her parents made no attempt to get along with her or be friendly and nice to her until she agreed to stop seeing John, their actions alone were not enough. Nancy needed to be convinced that it was in her own best interests to quit dating him. She came to realize that it might be necessary to separate from her family altogether if she continued to see him, and she decided that her family was more important. She also came to realize that John's possessiveness of her might prevent her from developing skills that could help her in the future. When she understood better the situation she was in, she could make her own decisions. The younger adolescent who acts out responds more easily to limit setting by itself, without needing to be convinced *why* she should change her behavior. With the older adolescent, excessive force from her parents without logical persuasion may not stop the girl's acting out; on the contrary, it can create more distance between the girl and her parents and cause her to act out even more.

In the next case, Evette's father seemed to see his daughter's choice of a boyfriend as impulsive acting out, while the girl felt that this behavior—her choice—was consistent with her identity. Evette was almost eighteen when her father called to make an appointment for her. He talked about his daughter's depression and anxiety and about her boyfriend, whom he felt might be part of the problem. He said that it did not matter to him that Evette's boyfriend was black, but he was concerned because the boy came from a culture so different from his daughter's. He would have preferred that she find another young man; Evette, as the therapist later learned, wanted help to develop a sense of mastery over her fears and her inability to live away from home.

Evette came in for her therapy sessions very willingly. She said that actually it was her idea to seek psychotherapy; her father had simply wanted to make the appointment. She complained of feeling anxious and depressed. She related that she was born with a congenital heart problem and that she was under a doctor's care continuously when she was young; surgery for the condition had to be delayed until she was older. Of the three children in the family (she had an older brother and a younger sister), she was her father's favorite; since she could not be physically active as a young child, she and her father had spent a lot of time together. Even until quite recently, they talked at length almost every evening and discussed many things, especially politics. Her father was a local politician noted for his charisma. Evette liked and respected him.

Evette was living at home. She had gone away to college briefly but became so homesick that she dropped out of school and returned. Although she had considered going to school locally or finding a job near home, she was too frightened to try either.

Evette talked of her boyfriend Barry, whom she loved and thought she might marry. Barry was loving and attentive. They spent many hours together talking about many things. Evette counseled Barry about getting a job; she thought that a job with a large company might offer better chances for advancement. He, in turn, encouraged her to go back to school while she still had the opportunity. They were very dependent on each other, each helping the other face the world.

Evette saw her therapist weekly for about six months and used the sessions to make plans for her future; she also became very dependent on her therapist. Despite her fears, she found a job as a typist and signed up for a night class at a local junior college. She continued to see Barry, who had found a job as a computer operator in a large firm. Using Evette's advice on how to be persuasive in an interview, Barry convinced his employers that he could be trusted in spite of once being arrested when he was a juvenile. Evette wanted to move out of her parents' home, but the prospect frightened her. It took considerable thinking through since she had not done well when she went away to college. During the sessions, Evette discussed her fears and her tentative plans for moving out. Because of her success at her job, her talks with Barry, and her psychotherapy, Evette gained self-confidence and developed some coping skills and a greater sense of mastery. Still, the thought of leaving home continued to frighten her.

Evette's father became increasingly angry with her. He really wanted his daughter to stop seeing Barry, yet he felt that he could not tell her so. He hinted but never expressed himself directly; Evette knew, of course. He was so disagreeable when Barry came to the house that Barry stopped visiting Evette there. Evette explained to her therapist that her father probably found it difficult to complain about Barry after his many years of supporting liberal political causes and pushing for opportunities for minorities. Since her father's anger was apparent to everyone at home, she felt she must move out and started to plan to get her own apartment.

Evette did move out. To accomplish her goal of leaving home, she needed to increase her feelings of self-confidence, and therapy helped. The unbearable tensions around the house, created by her father's anger, also motivated her move.

Evette had acted out by finding a boyfriend whom her father could not accept. Although her father put a great deal of pressure on Evette to stop seeing Barry, he could not get her to change her mind. When Evette was younger, any such overt display of displeasure by her father always resulted in Evette doing what he wanted. But this time he could not convince her that he was truly concerned about her own good. It was his wish, for his convenience, not hers. Evette proceeded to do what she felt was best for herself.

Another interesting aspect in this case was the closeness, mutual love, and respect between father and daughter—which was so comfortable for both that it was difficult for Evette to become independent. In Barry she found a man who overtly seemed quite different from her father; he did not have the charisma, the education, or the position in the community that her father did—and he was of another race. However, in the aspects most important to Evette, Barry and her father had much in common. Both loved her dearly and were very attentive, and both liked to have long talks with her. When a girl and her father have been so close and when the relationship has been so mutually satisfactory, the girl's separation can be problematic—either the girl or the father or both may act out at this time. Evette's choice of a lover that embarrassed her father may have been such acting out. At any rate, she succeeded in separating from her father, but it was a mutually painful experience.

Eliana's case concerns an older adolescent girl who, years earlier, had accepted the identity of a delinquent. Psychotherapy allowed her an opportunity to modify her behavior and her identity, but she herself had to make the decision to change. Eliana, a seventeen-year-old Mexican-American, was referred for psychotherapy by one of the counselors of a youth drop-in center that Eliana frequented. Eliana had come to the center intoxicated one day and had run from the building into the street, directly into the path of a passing car. She was hit and suffered many bruises and a broken leg. The counselor was concerned about Eliana's drinking but more concerned about her apparent self-destructive tendencies.

In the first psychotherapy sessions, Eliana seemed immediately to enjoy the attention the situation offered her. Although she expressed a strong interest in weekly sessions, she was not comfortable enough with the psychotherapist to reveal much about herself for several weeks. She said she was the second of six children, but the eldest living child. Several years earlier, the older girl had been killed in an automobile accident when she and the mother were returning from taking the father to a residential drug center for treatment of his heroin addiction. Eliana's family was a multiproblem family. Her father was currently in jail because he had stabbed a man in a street fight. The two eldest boys had been placed out of the home by the juvenile court. The family was on welfare, but her mother earned money occasionally by doing housework.

Eliana eventually reported that she had been drinking heavily in binges for several years and that she had been drinking daily for the past several months. She complained of having a great deal of difficulty with her boyfriend, Michael. She frequently left Michael's home intoxicated and angry and wandered the streets looking for a fight. Michael made her so angry. He was never nice to her anymore. He criticized her mercilessly, even in front of their friends. He would take Eliana into the bedroom to have sex with him while their friends listened and waited in the living room, and then he would angrily ask her to leave. Eliana stated that although Michael was one of her main problems she also had difficulty getting along with her mother. She complained that her mother did not seem to like her and never spent much time with her—in contrast to Michael's mother, who was kind and talked with her. Eliana was very dependent on her therapist and seemed hungry for attention and affection.

In her psychotherapy sessions, Eliana tried to figure out why her mother disliked her so much. Actually, her mother never seemed to like three of her six children: the daughter who had died, Eliana, and the eldest son. She seemed to like the younger three children better; she talked with them more and also took them along when she went somewhere. Eliana wondered if her mother disliked the eldest three because of their appearance—they looked more Chicano, like the father. The mother was not of Mexican descent and had a fair complexion and light hair, as did the younger three children.

The psychotherapist asked the mother to come in with Eliana for one of the sessions and questioned her about any problems with Eliana. The mother turned out to be an extremely inarticulate woman. She could hardly express herself and reminded the therapist of someone with severe learning disabilities or partial aphasia. The therapist felt that this woman could hardly be the talkative, friendly mother Eliana wanted; she must have found it difficult to have long talks with anyone. She did tell Eliana in the joint interview that she wished Eliana would find another boyfriend. She said she knew it must be Eliana's decision since no one could tell a woman whom she should love, not even her mother. She added that she loved Eliana's father very much, but that she had married him despite strong opposition from her own mother, who still would not allow Eliana's father into the house. The mother said she realized that love meant a lot, but that it surely was helpful if one's husband worked and supported his family and was responsible. She feared that Eliana would soon marry Michael and be in much the same situation as she, herself, had been all these years. Her message to Eliana was quite touching, and Eliana was impressed.

Eliana was still not convinced, however, that she should stop seeing Michael, but she was soon after him to find a job. He repeatedly promised her that he would, and Eliana, of course, believed him. But in her sessions, Eliana began complaining even more about the way Michael treated her. She made some attempts to break off their relationship, but Michael always won her back, usually by threatening to beat up any man who came near her. That frightened Eliana; she feared she would end up with *no* boyfriend.

Eventually, with the support of her therapist, Eliana decided to stop seeing Michael once and for all. Although she did not find another boyfriend immediately, she did find some girls to socialize with, and occasionally she dated other young men. She was much less depressed. She graduated from high school and entered a vocational rehabilitation training program because she felt that she could not get a good job without having such training first.

Eliana ended her psychotherapy after she became involved in the training program but returned to see the therapist twice: once six months after termination and then four months after that. She did not have a specific problem she wanted to talk about; rather, she seemed to want the therapist to see how well she was doing. At the time of her last visit, she was living with a new boyfriend who was nice to her and who had a job. She was not drinking except for a rare social drink and was not wandering the streets looking for fights. If all went well, she felt she might marry her new boyfriend in another six months.

Eliana used her psychotherapy time well. She came to realize that her relationship with Michael was demeaning and destructive for her. It took time for her to believe that this was true; she could not simply take her mother's words as good advice. She had been acting out by drinking, fighting, and dating Michael for several years. She needed to decide for herself that her behavior was self-destructive. When she did, she altered her behavior and quit seeing Michael. She had sufficient control over her actions to change when she felt that it was necessary for her to do so.

The pervasive tendency of the adolescent to become very dependent on the psychotherapist can be observed in Eliana's case. Eliana wanted to please her therapist, and the dependency allowed the therapist to influence her. Eliana even became somewhat possessive of the therapist, not liking it when she discovered that another girl at the adolescent drop-in center was seeing the same therapist. The situation probably reminded her of having to compete with five siblings for her mother's attention.

Lana is an example of an older adolescent who had developed an identity quite different from the "straight," middle-class identity of her parents and siblings. A seventeen-year-old Chinese-American girl, Lana was the third of four children in an up-

wardly mobile family. Her parents and her siblings strongly es-
poused the ethic of getting ahead in the world. Her two sisters
were already in college, and her younger brother hoped to go to
college on an athletic scholarship. Lana had been getting into
trouble ever since she started high school. She did well academically, but she ran away from home numerous times. She used
street drugs excessively and argued with her parents continuously.
On two occasions, she was placed in group homes by the juvenile
probation department, but in both places she refused to obey the
rules.

Lana was referred for psychotherapy by her probation officer because he felt she had self-destructive tendencies. Lana was
skeptical but curious when she arrived for her first appointment.
She was seductively but expensively dressed. She stated that she
had just returned home after living by herself in a downtown
apartment. Her parents had paid the rent, but otherwise she had
supported herself. She worked full time in an office and part time
in an all-night coffee shop. On the advice of her probation officer, she returned home after being raped by a man who had kidnapped her from a downtown shopping area. She told her story
about the rape with much anguish and complained that the
police did not believe her because of her juvenile court record.
She was still trying to get the district attorney to bring charges
against the man. Although she had come to fear living alone, she
was again experiencing the difficulties that had made her want to
leave home in the first place. Her parents were always angry with
her because she did not dress and act as they felt she should. Occasionally, they would call her a whore or a prostitute under their
breath. She was spending as little time with them as possible, and
her parents complained to her probation officer that Lana was
cold and indifferent to them and that they found it difficult to
have her at home.

When she was living on her own, Lana secretly associated
with a pimp and a few of his friends, although she was not sexually involved with any of them. She was determined to lead a
"clean" life until she turned eighteen, and then she intended to
become a prostitute with a select clientele.

Lana's escapade with the man who kidnapped and raped her

was perhaps unavoidable. However, the psychotherapist said that she wondered how it could be possible for a girl who had been able to live on her own not to be suspicious of the man from the outset. There were two other times, while she was in therapy, that Lana put herself into positions of danger. Her therapist pointed out that both incidents followed arguments with her parents in which they had again berated her. Lana doubted that there were any connections between her parents berating her and her putting herself into positions of danger, but she did say that there were times when she wished she were dead—usually after one of her parents told her how awful she was.

Lana remembered that when she was a child her mother frequently beat her. Her mother apparently had attacks of uncontrollable rage, and Lana seemed to be the most frequent victim of those rages. Sometimes she was even beaten for her brother's or sister's wrongdoings because she interceded to rescue them. These beatings, which had her father's tacit approval (he did not stop his wife), were the foundations for Lana's low self-esteem. If her mother did not like her, who could? The verbal beratings she was still receiving from both of her parents reinforced her negative self-image. Since Lana, as a child, put herself in a position to take punishment for her siblings, it might appear that she really liked to suffer. Actually, she was giving her mother one more chance to show if she really cared for her daughter. If she did not beat her, the mother would be sending a message Lana really wanted to hear—that her mother did love her after all. Unfortunately, Lana never got the communication she wanted; she just received more beatings. There was a strong possibility that Lana, as a seventeen-year-old, put herself into potentially dangerous situations as a sort of test: would she be harmed or wouldn't she? If she were not harmed, "mother nature" or "dame fate" would be telling her that she was a worthwhile person. Lana's lack of suspiciousness that facilitated her being kidnapped and raped was a test of this sort. Even though she never seemed to get the answer she wanted, Lana tried time and time again to somehow come to feel she was worthwhile; these attempts were the basis for her self-destructive tendencies.

Lana saw the therapist for less than six months, terminating before her eighteenth birthday. In this short time, she did not come to understand herself to any great extent. However, she did acknowledge the possibility of self-destructive tendencies and accepted that these tendencies might have something to do with her parents' strong disapproval of her and her life-style. She learned to watch for and guard against self-destructive moves. Enough modification of her ego ideal occurred in her psychotherapy so that, although she still did not approve of herself, she did not feel it was necessary to destroy herself—an attitude that hopefully will help her in the future.

Lana had a very firmly fixed identity, and psychotherapy was not helpful in changing that identity. However, it was helpful in getting Lana to recognize a symptom that might be a problem for her and one that she wanted to change: her self-destructive tendencies. The older adolescent with a formed identity of delinquency will not modify her behavior unless she is convinced that she wants to. Lana did not wish to change her whole life-style, and she did not do so.

The cases presented in this chapter demonstrate that outpatient psychotherapy can be helpful with many older adolescent girls who act out. Successfully handling such girls differs from effectively managing younger girls. Although the older girl can be encouraged to desist behaving as she has been if some limits or deterrents are used, limit setting alone is not appropriate. The older girl needs to be convinced through some logical, rational method that her behavior eventually causes her to lose a great deal, that it is self-demeaning or self-destructive, or that in some other way it is not in her own best interests. The older girl has more self-control and, if convinced to do so, she will help to control her own behavior. One factor to keep in mind in treating any patient is the identity the patient has developed. This is especially important to remember when treating the older girl since she has a more focused identity than the younger adolescent—a fact often overlooked. Failing to make such an assessment can lead to a therapeutic failure.

In office treatment of the older adolescent, the therapist should offer only the help the girl is asking for or that she can be enticed to request; help cannot be forced on her. Occasionally, when outpatient treatment seems futile, arrangements can be made for the girl to enter a residential treatment setting or a psychiatric hospital. If such a residential program is deemed necessary for longer than just a short period, a peer-confrontation program should be considered, since this type of setting, in my opinion, is most helpful for the adolescent patient.

Drug-abuse programs such as Synanon and Delancy Street (Yablonsky, 1965; Bourne and Ramsen, 1975) were among the first treatment programs to use the peer-confrontation philosophy. When working with the addict population, one is dealing with a subculture where secrecy and clandestine activities are intimately associated with the drug abuse itself. Yet one addict usually knows when another addict is again using drugs or when that person is facing problems that can lead to further drug use. Residential drug-treatment programs give the addict a great deal of responsibility for exposing the drug use and problems of other addicts. Such programs attempt to bring more problems into the open where they can be dealt with in group counseling sessions than might otherwise be possible. The same principle has been adapted for use in residential treatment settings for adolescents with drug-abuse problems, a history of delinquency, or mental illness. Such programs must be tailored to the maturity of the adolescent and to the seriousness of the mental illness. A regressed, psychotic adolescent cannot tolerate the degree of confrontation that the drug-abusing or delinquent youngster could handle fairly comfortably, but even the "sickest" patient can profit from learning how others react to his behavior.

Group confrontation has been successful in such residential situations as the juvenile hall (Lamb, 1973). Most of the adolescents admitted to juvenile halls are facing a crisis. Yet, since part of the philosophy or ethic of the delinquent subculture is not to trust adults in authority and not to "snitch" on one's peers, it can be almost impossible for the adult supervisors to help a troubled adolescent. If a peer-confrontation type of program can be established within a juvenile hall setting, the delinquent code of not "snitching" can be turned around and the adolescent can be encouraged to talk about the behavior and especially about the problems of other adolescents.

Having been involved in setting up such a program in a girls' unit of a juvenile hall, I have had an opportunity to see the effectiveness of peer confrontation. The girls in this program came to be able to confront each other about current behavior they found irritating and difficult to live with, but, in addition, the girls confronted each other about ineffective approaches to problem solving. The girls were quite willing, for example, to talk about how one girl could deal with her parents and offered suggestions that might help. They were also willing to talk about their boyfriends and the problems of their relationships. The only subject that appeared to be taboo, a subject about which the girls would not give advice, was pregnancy. They seemed to feel that what a girl decided to do about her pregnancy was a very personal matter and not a fit subject for group discussion. They were, of course, willing to listen to a girl trying to decide whether to have her baby or to have an abortion and were quite supportive in such situations. Since pregnancy is a very personal matter, it does not seem odd that the girls would not offer advice on what another girl should do.

The peer-confrontation process utilizes the natural tendencies of adolescents to confront each other about their behavior (Offer, 1969). Such confrontation by one's peers encourages the normal adolescent to conform to the usual way of dressing and of handling situations. If, for example, a girl comes to school wearing a new T-shirt or sweater and her friend says to her, "Oh, you have one of those new T-shirts," and says no more, the first girl will probably ask her friend if she likes the new shirt. If her friend answers with an unenthusiastic "sure," but later asks the girl if she has a pair of pants that would match the T-shirt, the first girl will begin to wonder whether or not she has worn the right outfit. She may be embarrassed and wear a jacket over her shirt for the rest of the day. Perhaps the confrontation will not be this gentle. A girl could come to school wearing her new T-shirt and be asked by her friend, "Why are you wearing those two things together? That looks dumb!" In any event, the girl has learned something about how one is "supposed" to dress.

Teenagers will also confront one another about their behavior. If one girl tells her friend about her troubles with her mother,

her friend will probably be sympathetic. But her friend may also ask, "Don't you think that you could have explained things to your mother better? If she really knew why we all were coming home late, don't you think she would be less angry?" An adolescent girl does give her friends advice about dealing with parents, with other girls, and with boys also. Peer-confrontation programs use the adolescent's natural way of relating to others in a therapeutic setting.

Group-confrontation programs seem to be most effective in a residential setting. When girls live together, they will come to know a great deal about the others. Central to the concept of a group-confrontation program are the daily counseling sessions in which each resident is encouraged to discuss any conflicts, problems, or temptations she is facing and any conflicts, problems, or temptations she has learned that other group members are facing. All members of the group are responsible for talking about their problems and those that others are facing.

In setting up such a group-confrontation program, the staff must establish a reward system for the adolescent who participates in the confrontation process. Rewarding a girl with more privileges, since she has assumed more responsibility, can motivate the other girls to participate. The staff of such a program must be sincerely interested in helping the adolescents, for teenagers are especially adept at ferreting out hypocrisy.

Such a group-confrontation program should be considered for the older acting-out adolescent who is seriously self-destructive and unable to relate to a psychotherapist in individual therapy. Her peers may be able to help her see what she will gain by altering her behavior.

SIX

Problems of Transference and Countertransference

A younger adolescent unable to control her self-destructive acting-out behavior may come to view her psychotherapist as extremely powerful. Seeing her therapist as powerful and capable of controlling her helps the girl limit her behavior. She can, to some extent, ease her fears of becoming out of control. It is as if her magical, omnipotent therapist will take care of her and protect her from her own hostile and self-destructive impulses, even when the therapist is not around. After such a transference has developed, the amount of acting out actually does diminish. The girl acts out less because she feels that her therapist is preventing her from doing so; or, knowing that her therapist disapproves of certain behavior, she fears he or she will find out and "do something." It is usually not clear just what her therapist will "do" about the behavior, but the psychotherapist is usually seen as an awesome but benevolent controller.

For want of a better term, I use *transference* to describe the view of an omnipotent therapist that the younger, out-of-control adolescent girl sometimes develops. The therapist obviously does not possess magical powers, nor does he or she attempt to make the patient believe that he or she has such capabilities: the patient's view is entirely her own perception of the therapist — her transference. Normally, when one observes transference in the adult patient or even in the older adolescent girl, one notices quite a bit of displacement. The patient transfers to or displaces on the therapist feelings, usually from childhood, she had toward some significant person or persons in her life. For example, if she had had a hostile and dependent relationship with her mother, she could transfer these feelings to her therapist and try to establish a similar hostile, dependent relationship with the therapist. Or, if, as a child, the patient had been very frightened of her father, she might see her therapist similarly and act as if she were frightened of him — or of *her,* since such displacement can occur regardless of the sex of the therapist. The patient is unaware of what is happening; it is unconscious. When the younger adolescent girl who lacks controls sees her therapist as omnipotent, she does so because she needs to feel someone is in charge of her impulsivity. The transference she develops is not the same as the older person's displacement of feelings but is an outgrowth of her needs at this particular time in her life.

Of course, not all adolescent girls develop this view of an omnipotent therapist. Such transference seems to occur only in the younger adolescent and usually after the therapist has needed to set limits on the girl's behavior several times. With a loss of privileges, such a transference can develop. Or, perhaps the therapist stops a girl who is in out-patient psychotherapy just as she is about to behave in a self-destructive manner by imposing some restrictions. The transference probably is an exaggeration of the feelings of constraint and control she experienced as a result of the limitations on her behavior. Transference does not develop unless the girl sees her therapist as a strong person, capable of handling out-of-control situations. She must also feel that the therapist has her best interests at heart and that the restrictions and control over her behavior are not being exercised out of anger. Ideally, the therapist should be able to take charge of the situation, set limits on the girl's behavior, and react with little or no anger to the frustrations of the task or to the girl's verbal abuse and resistance. Doing so is not always possible, but a therapist must learn to recognize and then control his or her frustrations so that the girl will see the limit setting for what it is—and not as angry retaliation or punishment for her actions.

If the parents of the younger adolescent are somewhat inhibited around the therapist, transference to a person seen as magical and omnipotent is more likely to develop. The girl already thinks of her parents as having power over her, and now since the psychotherapist can intimidate her parents it must mean that the therapist possesses even greater power. The older adolescent, generally more thoughtful, has less blind faith than the younger girl, and thus she is less likely to develop a view of her therapist as omnipotent.

In the earlier chapter on limit setting, the case of Cindy was mentioned—the girl who did not cooperate with her treatment and yet refused to leave the hospital. She was the one who said that if her new therapist grew on her it would be "like a fungus." After the therapist set some limits on her behavior while she was in the hospital, Cindy started to perceive her as having great power that could prevent her from acting out. She started feeling that her therapist knew when she was just thinking about acting out. It took Cindy about two weeks of experiencing the limits the therapist had set before she felt comfortable enough to be discharged from the hospital. When her behavior was controlled, her fears eased and she could leave. Even later, in the course of weekly psychotherapy, Cindy feared acting out between her sessions. She was sure her therapist could find out if she did not behave appropriately and would "do something." Although she expressed this sentiment several times in her therapy hours, she could never pinpoint exactly what she felt her therapist was going to do if she acted out.

Cindy's psychotherapist contributed to the transference by setting limits on the girl's behavior while she was in the hospital.

About six months after she was discharged, Cindy ran away from home and was gone two days and nights; she was found in a wooded park area where she had spent the entire time alone. At this point in her treatment, Cindy was beginning to recognize some of her dependency on her mother, which scared her. Also, newspaper stories about a man who had raped several victims in the area were making most females, including Cindy, exceedingly apprehensive. Together with her internal fears of not being able to sever her dependency on her mother, these frightening stories triggered, once again, Cindy's counterphobic acting out—she spent those two days alone in a desolate area as if she feared nothing. She again needed to be stopped. After Cindy was located, her therapist told her parents that they should ask the officers who found Cindy to take her to the juvenile hall as a runaway—not to bring her directly home. The therapist helped to make the necessary arrangements. This action undoubtedly increased or renewed the girl's view that the therapist had great powers. Again, the therapist had set limits on Cindy's behavior.

Cindy referred to her therapist as "the bomb." Although she rarely called her that in the therapy sessions, she always addressed the many notes she wrote "To the bomb." Cindy seemed to feel that her urges and drives to act out were so powerful that only someone or something as powerful as a bomb could stop her. Cindy's long notes described how she felt, and she would slip them under the therapist's office door during the night (Cindy lived very close to the office). Sometimes these notes were written in a laboriously small script; other times Cindy would sketch out how she felt with pen and ink, creating intricate, geometric drawings. By spending so much time on these notes and drawings and by "sending" them to her therapist at any time during the night, Cindy was contributing to her own perception of an omnipresent therapist. It was almost as though she could communicate with her therapist any time she wished or needed to, as though her therapist were always nearby. Many of Cindy's energies were diverted into communicating with the therapist rather than in acting out.

Somewhere near the end of the first year of therapy, Cindy's transference changed. One day in her therapy session, she seemed reluctant to talk. She mentioned some of the trouble she was having in her chemistry course. To encourage the conversation, the therapist said that she could really sympathize since she too had had a hard time in an organic chemistry course. That night, Cindy left this message under the therapist's door: "Somehow all of a sudden you look human, and not so damned formidable! i approve (bang, bang, bang, bang, bang)." With this note she exploded her myth. Her therapist seemed omnipotent no longer.

At the time she exploded the mystical view she had created of the therapist, Cindy had more self-control. She no longer needed to feel that someone else was protecting and intimidating her to prevent her self-destructive acting out. She now needed "regular" therapy—without strong internal controls from the therapist—to help her with her basic problems.

After that point in her therapy, Cindy talked about her fears rather than her bravery, especially her problems of relating to her peers and the social discomfort she felt. She feared that without her mother's help she could not handle things. She thought her father also felt this way, since he seemed to make no decisions; the mother made them all. She feared that no young man could possibly be interested in her unless she offered him sex immediately, and then she feared she would not know whether it was her or the sex that he liked. She was working on mastering her problems and insecurities, and she remained very dependent on her therapist. Now, however, she no longer felt her therapist was unnaturally powerful.

In Cindy's case, an adolescent girl could not come to deal with her problems until her acting-out behavior was stopped, or at least reduced. After the initial limit-setting process, Cindy became very dependent on her therapist and was intimidated by her. This dependency was renewed when limits were again applied when she was an out-patient. If her therapist had not been willing to actively set limits from the outset, the therapy probably would not have been successful. The inactive, neutral, psycho-analytic stance, which works so well with the comparatively healthy adult who seeks insight into his or her emotional responses, would have been quite useless in Cindy's case. Her first therapist had attempted to deal with her in this manner, and Cindy only became more angry and her control over her anger and impulsivity was reduced even more. She needed an active, flexible therapist who would take a stand against her self-destructive behavior and who was temporarily willing to take charge of her life. She needed a therapist who was an adult and who acted like one. The "buddy-buddy" approach was not what Cindy needed.

At a recent meeting, a therapist who works with adolescents talked anecdotally about an incident in a session with a fourteen-year-old girl. This girl had, after only two visits, told her that she felt she was so skillful a therapist that she could, undoubtedly, cure King Kong. One can assume from this statement that the girl felt that she, herself, had dreadful, animallike urges and that she hoped she had found a psychotherapist who could cure her.

Another example of transference to an "all-powerful" therapist can be seen in the case of Penny, a fourteen-year-old who came to the emergency room of a general hospital following a mild overdose of tranquilizers. The tranquilizers had been prescribed a week earlier by a physician who had seen her after Penny had impulsively run to the county children's receiving home asking to live there. She claimed she needed a place to live because her home and her mother were so bad. The following day, she disclaimed any knowledge as to why she did such a thing; she had a nice home and she had a nice mother.

Penny had taken the overdose of tranquilizers very impulsively, and later she stated that she had no reason to want to die. She stated that a "person" or a "devil" inside of her had made her overdose. It was not her idea to take the pills; the "person" said she must. During the two weeks preceding the overdose, Penny had also impulsively set several fires in her bedroom. An examination of Penny in the emergency room revealed that the girl had used a razor blade to scratch the word *HELP* on one forearm and *DANGER* on the other. She again disclaimed that it was her idea; the "devil" inside of her made her do so — and also to set the fires.

Penny, overtly fearful, was admitted to the psychiatric unit of the hospital. Her hair hung down over her face and she cowered in the corner of the patients' lounge. She spoke in breathless whispers and answered questions in monosyllables or short phrases. Her temperature was slightly elevated, as were her pulse and blood pressure. It was thought that this elevation in her vital signs was in response to intense fear. She admonished the psychiatrist to stay away from her because she too might be harmed by the "devil." She claimed it was dangerous to be near her.

Penny was the oldest of four children and the only girl. Her father deserted the family when Penny was eleven years old, and Penny's life changed considerably after that. Her father had been a charismatic man and very entertaining when he had spent time with the children. After he left, her mother was away from home a great deal and often left the children unsupervised — which gave Penny the opportunity to run around at night with other adolescents, intoxicated and destroying things like a pack of animals. She used and abused drugs and alcohol from the age of twelve. She was truant so often and argued with the school authorities so much that she was suspended indefinitely. When together, she and her mother argued continuously and ended up in shouting matches.

After a few sessions with the therapist in the hospital, which sometimes took place alone and sometimes with her mother present, Penny asked if the therapist had any special powers. She said her mother talked differently to the therapist than to most people. Seeing her mother's inhibition, Penny all the more easily came to view her therapist as unusually powerful.

After about a five-week stay in the hospital, Penny continued with weekly office psychotherapy. She still asked the therapist occasionally if she were magical. She seemed to continue to need to see her therapist as omnipotent. Despite such answers as "No, I have no magic, but I want to do all I can to help," Penny still would ask her therapist if she could read her mind. Or, she would ask if the therapist had stopped her from getting herself in trouble the past week. Once she was sure that her therapist had two nurses following her around all week; she had noticed two women and had thus been afraid to do anything wrong. Frequently her questioning was related to some acting out or a strong temptation to do something self-destructive, such as abuse drugs or stay out all night wandering the streets and parks alone.

Penny's hospital admission picture of bizarre behavior and thoughts, along with her suspiciousness and feelings of being controlled, could have been interpreted as psychosis in this young adolescent. However, in the two years of her treatment, the therapist saw no evidence that Penny was schizophrenic.

About six weeks after her discharge from the hospital, Penny swallowed about six of her mother's Valium tablets and showed up at the adolescent day treatment program intoxicated on the medication. She was again fearful of the "devil" inside her and very fearful of her mother. Her behavior was so impulsive and erratic that she was brought to the hospital for overnight observation.

Her mother, when she arrived, was angry that her tranquilizers had been consumed. She did not appear frightened that the tablets might have harmed her daughter or upset that her daughter might be suicidal — she was just angry that her pills were gone. After talking with the therapist, the mother calmed down and started behaving as a concerned parent. After her mother showed up, Penny became very upset and agitated; she appeared extremely frightened and tried to run off. She had to be stopped since she might have harmed herself in her angry, intoxicated, self-destructive state. She required physical restraints that were applied by the nursing staff, with the help of the therapist. (Actually, the therapist's help was more symbolic than real.) She was given a dose of a liquid concentrate tranquilizer. This medication was selected so that she would not be sedated too quickly and would thus have an opportunity to vent her rage, which she did. She shouted and cried for about an hour until she fell asleep. A nurse sat quietly in her room all night to make sure she was all right. Early the next morning, the therapist came to the hospital to release the girl from the restraints, with the help of the nursing staff, of course. After an interview, Penny was sent to school.

Penny now saw her therapist as part of the restraining-releasing process, since this was, indeed, what had happened. And Penny again saw the therapist influence her mother. The whole incident undoubtedly reinforced her seeing the therapist as unusually powerful since that person had actually stopped Penny's self-destructive acting out. Even though the therapist's actions increased the transference, it was appropriate to do so. At that point, Penny was not able to manage on her own; the increased transference gave her the external control and support she needed.

About a year after treatment started, Penny again asked her therapist whether or not she possessed magical powers. She had asked the same question many times before, and seemed to disregard negative answers. This time, Penny calmly said that she was glad to hear that the therapist was not magical but added that she had often thought so in the past. The subject never came up again. Penny was doing fairly well not only in school but also socially, and she no longer needed magic on her side. Now she needed a therapist who could help her understand her troubles. Her behavior was reasonably well controlled.

The main theme of the next phase of treatment was Penny's relationship with her mother. Penny complained about her mother regularly—that she was so often away and left Penny to care for her brothers, that her mother would come home to leave money for groceries but immediately leave again. Frequently Penny was disappointed because her mother would not be at home when she had promised, and consequently Penny could not go hiking with her friends. Her mother also embarrassed Penny by the way she dressed. Penny felt that her mother wore clothes too young for her and that she was too sloppy. Her mother's boyfriend also embarrassed Penny since he was so much younger. Penny's anger toward her mother consumed a great deal of energy.

Although she insisted she was terribly angry with her mother, Penny refused to live with a relative. At one point, her social worker found a foster family, as Penny had requested. At the last minute, however, Penny refused to leave her mother's home, saying that this was the only home and the only family she had and she did not wish to go anywhere else.

Penny seemed to have no alternative than to learn to adjust to her mother; her mother was not about to change. In the early phase of treatment, the therapist tried to help Penny see that she was, indeed, angry with her mother and that this anger, and not the "devil" inside of her, caused her to behave as she did. In this phase of her treatment, Penny's therapist tried to show her that she often set herself up to be hurt by her mother. Penny was told that if she did not expect her mother to be attentive, kind, and loving but instead accepted that her mother was neither giving nor maternal, then her mother could not hurt or disappoint her. Initially Penny resisted this view, but eventually she came to accept the idea. She would frequently catch herself expecting her mother to be a "storybook-perfect" mother and then had to stop to tell herself that this could never be. Her anger toward her mother eventually decreased. They were not close, but they were less angry with each other. They could live together until Penny was ready to leave home.

Since Penny's psychotherapy was being covered by Medicaid, the sessions had to terminate rather abruptly when authorization from the health care program was withdrawn. Penny was sad and said that she would miss her therapist, but she felt that she could manage without psychotherapy. Her behavior was appropriate, and she knew she could keep it that way. She also knew that she had successfully adjusted to her mother.

At the time of termination, Penny gave the therapist an interesting gift—a succulent plant from the desert, which she said had special healing powers. If one were to break off a piece of the plant and rub it on a wound, the wound would heal very rapidly. "Magic" still held a certain fascination for Penny—but this is certainly not out of the ordinary for an adolescent girl.

Giovacchini (1973) writes about a deficiency in the executive functions of the ego in borderline adolescents. Persons with this condition, he feels, have great difficulty with the adjustments they must make in their lives. When they cannot handle a situation, they feel that they have failed and their self-esteem is reduced. With less self-esteem, they are even less capable of handling the demands they face. He observed, in relation to a borderline person, "In the transference during psychotherapy, it becomes apparent that the patient is seeking an omnipotent sustaining relationship that will rescue him from the hateful, destructive aspects of his inner self" (pp. 271-272). he also states, "As the transference often reveals, patients suffering with characterological problems often assign omnipotent wisdom and goodness to the therapist and psychically fuse with him in order to gain sur-cease from their painful amorphous inner world" (p. 272).

The view of the therapist as omnipotent that can occur with the younger adolescent in psychotherapy is fraught with hazards. The psychotherapist may become uncomfortable with the great expectations placed on her and may wish to modify the trans-ference and interject a more realistic appraisal of herself *before* the girl is ready. It certainly can be uncomfortable to feel that one must live up to exaggerated expectations, and so the therapist may be tempted to try to alter the transference immediately. It is important to remember, however, that this transference is the girl's creation. The therapist did not advertise herself as having the power to perform omnipotent acts. If the therapist cannot prevent an adolescent girl from acting out in a self-destructive manner, the therapist has not failed to perform the "magic"—it is the girl's actions that are causative. If one has never promised a miracle, one cannot be blamed for not producing one. However, if a girl wishes to believe that her therapist can produce miracles because of her own needs, the therapist does not need to interject reality before the girl can accept it. Still, there is a danger that the psychotherapist will enjoy being admired as a godlike person and wish to maintain that image of herself in the eyes of her pa-tient. The life of a psychotherapist is not always as gratifying or as glamorous as one may have hoped, and such grandiose impres-sions expressed by a patient can indeed be pleasant.

Giovacchini (1973) warns: "During treatment there may be a reciprocal interaction between the patient and the therapist regarding the assignment of omnipotence. The therapist, usually unconsciously, accepts the assigned role projected onto him" (p. 273). This is a potentially dangerous situation. The therapist cannot indefinitely meet the needs of the patient, and so the pa-tient will eventually suffer another disappointment and the treat-ment will end unsuccessfully. However, while Giovacchini's cautions are to be heeded, I think that the therapist should occa-sionally allow such a transference—when it is clearly in the inter-ests of the patient and when it is clearly temporary—and not in-sist that the patient view the therapist more realistically until she is ready to do so. The therapist must eventually encourage the patient to alter her perception. Allowing the transference to remain when it is so desperately needed by the patient is, of course, quite different from the mutually satisfying misperception of reality shared by patient and therapist that Giovacchini describes.

In each of the cases mentioned in this chapter, the therapist was female. When the psychotherapist is male, sexual overtones can make the management of such a transference more complicated. This added complication should, of course, be considered in treating younger adolescent girls. It does not mean that all girls should be treated by female therapists or that male therapists should not allow this intense transference to develop. The sexual attraction and potential seductiveness of the adolescent girl is just another factor psychotherapists should consider.

In the above cases, the perception of the therapist's omnipotence may represent a transference in which the adolescent regresses to a much younger age and sees the therapist as she once saw her parents—as all-powerful and all-knowing compared to her tiny, vulnerable self. It does seem unusual, however, that such transference develops so rapidly. As we have seen, it can happen within a very few sessions. It is possible that what is occurring is not a true transference at all but an arrangement of convenience, perhaps a defense, since it so obviously serves to provide external controls for the adolescent who is not sufficiently able to control her own impulses.

In more common and less dramatic therapy relationships, the transference the adolescent girl appears to develop is a fairly straightforward dependency on the therapist. In this more common dependent relationship, the adolescent girl is generally agreeable and pleasant to the therapist and interested in the therapist's opinion about her clothes and activities, but she is even more interested in the therapist's opinion of her as a person. She seems to have a strong need to be liked and to have the therapist approve of her. Of course, the adolescent girl will be irritating at times and challenge the therapist, but she usually keeps her demeanor within the limits of the therapist's tolerance so as not to lose approval.

Perhaps the adolescent, in her growing independence and in her increasing concern over her own decision making, needs the approval of an adult, other than her own parents, whom she can trust and depend on. Although she may have had a satisfactory relationship with her parents earlier, she could realize that her parents find her growing independence difficult. Many parents have such difficulty, and they unwittingly withdraw their love, not fully approving of the new independence. Since the therapist will not withdraw support as the girl becomes more mature and self-reliant, temporary dependence on such a person may be extremely important for the adolescent. The therapist's and the girl's goals are similar in this respect.

Others have observed the dependency of the adolescent on the therapist. The GAP Report on Normal Adolescence (1968) observes, "Unable to remain closely dependent on his parents and considerably distressed emotionally, the adolescent . . . turns to others outside the immediate family for limits on his behavior, for guidance, and for identification. He forms transient, but often intense attachments and 'crushes' on a variety of adults" (p. 67). Aichorn (1964), in his essay on "Education in Training Schools," states that the development of dependent transference is necessary before "curative education" can begin. In this essay, he describes some of the therapeutic moves he made that encouraged strongly dependent transference in adolescent boys. Offer and Offer (1968), in their research investigation of six average adolescent girls whom they followed over a three-year period, found that five of the six very rapidly entered into a positive research alliance with the researcher. They observed that the average adolescent girl, even a girl not identified as a patient, becomes rapidly dependent on an interested adult. And Johnson (1949), in her essay "Sanctions for Superego Lacunae," stresses the need for a positive, dependent transference in the treatment of children and adolescents with superego lacunae, stating that such a transference allows the child to identify with a superego without such lacunae.

As mentioned earlier, in relation to transference to a person seen as magical, it is possible to view a strongly dependent relationship on the therapist as the adolescent's regression to a much younger age when she saw her parents as very strong and protective. But, here again, the positive, dependent relationship

develops so quickly and so often and with adolescents from vary-
ing family backgrounds that one wonders if it really is a regression. The element of displacement one usually sees in transference in adults seems to be missing. Perhaps one can look at this
strongly dependent relationship in terms of the need it serves.
The therapist could be the approving adult, a parent surrogate
who not only allows but also encourages the adolescent's increasing independence. An adolescent girl's self-esteem increases as
she becomes more independent and self-reliant, but she finds it
difficult to achieve this self-confidence without the approval of
the parent she depends on—or without a parent surrogate, that
is, the therapist.

An interesting thing happens with this strongly dependent
relationship. It can quickly dissipate and disappear with very little notice when the adolescent is ready to manage her life to her
own satisfaction. When the therapist is no longer needed, the
adolescent girl frequently "drops" her so rapidly that the therapist may wonder what has happened. Nothing may have "happened" except that the girl no longer needs the therapist so desperately; she is now so busy living her own life that she can hardly
wait to move on to the next phase. When an adolescent girl who
has made progress in psychotherapy suddenly decides to terminate, the therapist should thoughtfully consider whether therapy is still really necessary before attempting to continue the
therapy or to interpret the behavior to the girl as her desire to
avoid treatment. The therapist must be prepared to let go of the
relationship when doing so becomes the supportive and growth-
producing action the adolescent girl now needs.

An abrupt change in the girl's relationship with the therapist, an abrupt cessation of her strong dependency, an abrupt
reversal of her desperate need for approval—all can come as a
narcissistic blow to the therapist. The therapist may have been
enjoying (and needing) the attention of such a dependent, admir-
ing young patient too much.

A therapist who is uncomfortable with deviating from the
psychoanalytic model—which is characterized by relative inactivity on the part of the therapist and by its goal of producing insights in the patient—will probably be uncomfortable, and un-

successful, in treating adolescents. The role of the psychotherapist treating the adolescent must be an active one, with the therapist participating and sometimes initiating the conversations and interrupting the silences. The therapist must also be active in setting limits when necessary or in mobilizing the adolescent to try new approaches or activities that can help her gain more independence, self-assurance, and a sense of mastery.

Gittleson (1948), in his classic essay on character synthesis, stated, "Treatment may fail not because it is dynamically inaccurate but because it is emotionally inadequate. Complete objectivity is not enough. . . . Treatment that is concerned about the dynamics of the problem may fail because it disregards this fact. . . . Character synthesis, with the therapist as catalyst, synergist, and model, is the immediate goal in dealing with the problems of adolescence" (p. 430). To produce such character synthesis, the therapist needs to play many roles—not just the analyst of the dynamics. Many therapists find such roles difficult because of their emphasis on the science rather than the art of psychotherapy.

Sometimes treatment is influenced by the psychotherapist's *countertransference* to the patient. In such a situation, the therapist brings to the treatment situation feelings that she or he felt earlier for some significant person. The therapist may transfer or displace these feelings to the patient. For example, if the therapist has lost a child and now is seeing a child in psychotherapy of approximately the same age and the same sex as his dead child, it is possible for the therapist to displace or transfer to the patient feelings that he earlier felt for his child. The therapist could become so involved in seeing the patient as the lost child that he cannot let the patient be different. Or, if the therapist is treating a woman who has many of the same characteristics as her (the therapist's) mother, she might transfer to the patient feelings she formerly felt for her mother and, depending on the prior relationship, be either too solicitous or too intolerant of the patient.

A psychotherapist who feels that she or he missed much as a teenager and wishes to relive that era, or a therapist who feels that he or she is growing older, may—acting in countertransference—overidentify with the adolescent patient. Such would-be

therapists for adolescents are led to ignore the importance of psychodynamics and lose sight of therapy as a serious responsibility. I
am sure we have all seen such "therapists," fascinated by adolescent customs and manners, dress and act and talk like adolescents, insisting that doing so is valuable in their "therapy." They
justify their overidentification with the adolescents they treat by
saying that adolescents do not trust adults. Will, then, an adolescent trust an adult disguised as an adolescent? The type of therapist described is not usually concerned about psychodynamics but
instead feels that being a "buddy" to the patient will somehow
accomplish the "right" results.

Either overfascination and overidentification with the youthful patient or rigid adherence to the relatively inactive and in-
sight-producing role of the analytic stance can be viewed as countertransference when treating the adolescent patient. Overidentification and overfascination with the youthful patient could indicate that a therapist is trying to relive his or her youth vicariously
through the therapy situation. The rigidity of the pseudoanalytic
stance could be interpreted as the therapist's reaction to the intensity of the adolescent's drives and urges—behavior that makes
the therapist feel so uncomfortable that he or she has to take
refuge in a more traditional role.

A therapist who has not yet succeeded in dealing with his or
her own adolescence may develop a potentially destructive countertransference. Many therapists went through their adolescence
when it was not culturally acceptable to act out sexual and hostile
drives. Some therapists, remembering their desires to act out
more as adolescents, but who did not dare to do so at the time,
may vicariously enjoy the descriptions of the sexual escapades of
their patients or their direct expressions of anger toward their
parents, teachers, or other authority figures. Such therapists may
overtly or covertly urge their patients to act out more. Under the
guise of not being moralistic or judgmental, they are likely to
avoid setting appropriate limits on acting-out behavior because of
their own needs.

Meeks (1971), in discussing the positive and negative aspects
of having an adolescent patient treated by a young adult thera-

pist, is concerned that "although the young adult therapist might be closer in age to the patient and thus could legitimately share some of the adolescent patient's cultural interests, the young adult therapist's closeness to his own adolescent struggles might be a disadvantage since these struggles might be revived" (p. 32). Meeks feels that "the young adult lacks the security of personal identity that would allow him to view the adolescent's struggles from a perspective of tolerant understanding" (p. 32). I concur but also feel that not only the young adult therapist but also the therapist going through a mid-life crisis is likely to find that an adolescent patient revives his or her own adolescent struggles and yearnings.

Psychotherapy with an adolescent is not always fascinating and interesting. It can be long and tedious as the therapist helps the patient to recognize what she really feels and understand how these feelings developed. The task of helping the adolescent master the problems she faces can be a slow and often painstaking process. To do psychotherapy well with an adolescent girl, the therapist must be patient and recognize and reinforce small gains and advances.

The adolescent girl in psychotherapy needs a therapist who is an adult and who behaves as an adult. She needs a therapist who has worked through his or her own adolescence and has put it behind so that overidentification with adolescence or a vicarious reliving of adolescence will not adversely influence the course of therapy. She needs a therapist who is able to deviate from the psychoanalytic stance of neutrality and inactivity, which is designed to increase the transference and lead to insight. She needs a therapist who will be active in the therapy sessions and resourceful in finding ways to set limits on her behavior, if she needs them, or in suggesting approaches to help her learn to master her problems and fears. She needs a therapist whom she feels is strong enough to handle her intense feelings of depression or her strong urge to act out in a self-destructive or self-demeaning manner. She needs a therapist whom she feels can be depended on until she is ready to rely on herself. Since the adolescent girl may act out so much and be so perplexed by the many changes she faces, she can develop an intense transference to the therapist; in turn, her transference may evoke countertransference in the therapist, which could prevent the girl from getting what she needs. The psychotherapist who works with adolescent girls must vigilantly watch for this potential problem so that the psychotherapy can be successful.

SEVEN

Advising Parents

An inexperienced psychotherapist treating an adolescent girl will all too often look for and empathize with the mistakes and psychopathology of the parents—not a very constructive approach. It is more useful to assess the psychodynamics between the adolescent and her parents to determine what the girl needs at this point in her life. The next step is to tell the parents, to give them advice. The therapist should look at the present, the here and now, to find out what is necessary rather than at the past to uncover what mistakes the parents may have made. Instead of pointing out what they *should* have done, the therapist can advise them about what they can do now. If the therapist assumes this positive attitude, he or she will be better able to elicit the parents' aid.

If parents are sufficiently concerned about their daughter to willingly bring her for psychotherapy, one can assume that they will try to respond to advice and guidance from the therapist. They will probably be able to learn to relate to their daughter more effectively to help her overcome her symptoms and to promote her growing independence. It is usually unnecessary for the parents themselves to enter psychotherapy; conferences with the therapist will suffice to help the parents deal with their daughter more appropriately.

The psychotherapist's attitude toward the parents during a conference is extremely important. If the therapist really is committed to the positive approach, he or she will find that most parents can be told in a straightforward manner how to handle their daughter; hints, implicit messages, or lengthy explanations are not really necessary. If the therapist's attitude is helpful and supportive, she or he can also confront the parents directly about any inappropriate actions. If, after being confronted about what they are doing now, the parents try to go back and find their past mistakes, the psychotherapist should seriously consider interrupting this soul-searching and bring the parents back to the present. Only rarely—if the parents can look into the past without becoming unduly guilty, if they have had previous experience with psychotherapy, and if they seem to have good rapport with their daughter's therapist—should they be allowed to analyze the past, and then only tentatively. The emphasis should still be on what kinds of parents their daughter needs now.

Parents can be told, for example, that their daughter needs more limits on her behavior than they are now providing. Or, they can be told that she needs their approval or permission— in short, an opportunity—to make more of her own decisions, including the opportunity to fail. If the parents are hesitant to follow this advice, they will probably say so, and the ensuing discussion can be very fruitful. The parents will have a chance to explain why the advice poses difficulty for them, and they can learn more about themselves in the process. They can ask the therapist to clarify what she or he wishes them to do and why. Further, the therapist may decide to alter the advice after learning more about the parents' concerns.

Conferences with the parents can be done by the psychotherapist working with the adolescent girl or by another mental health professional. It has been my experience that holding conferences with the parents has not interfered with the general air of confidentiality and trust so necessary for the girl's psychotherapy. If one therapist has contact with both the adolescent and her parents, he or she is less likely to be critical of the parents for their past mistakes or insensitivities and more likely to give them constructive advice; the therapist will have a better understanding of the family's dynamics.

Parent-teacher conferences are common occurrences in most children's lives. The younger adolescent probably views conferences between her therapist and parents in the same way and is not as suspicious about such conferences as might be anticipated. Youngsters continue to trust and learn from their teachers after parent-teacher conferences; similarly, they will also continue to trust and confide in their therapists. Still, it is important for the adolescent girl to know when there is contact between her parents and her therapist. She should be told ahead of time, if at all possible; if not, she should be told at the first opportunity. Sometimes a parent will feel that it is imperative to call the therapist, and she may not have told her daughter she was going to make the phone call—thinking that it was not in the same category as a face-to-face, prearranged conference. Yet the daughter should also be informed before any telephone conversation. An adolescent patient appreciates knowing when her parents and her therapist are talking, and she may even be impressed that she is being told; she probably has assumed that a great deal more contact is occurring than is actually the case.

The adolescent patient can be given the general outline or nature of the topics discussed in a conference, if she asks. But she should not be given a precise rundown of who said what or a detailed picture of her parents' attitudes. If pushed to relate what her parents said about a certain subject, the psychotherapist can remind the girl that she would not like her parents to know exactly what *she* says in her sessions and that her parents have the same right to privacy. It is possible to discuss the girl with her parents or the parents with their daughter without revealing the secrets of either party.

If an adolescent girl expresses concern over an approaching parent conference, she can be asked if there is something in particular she does not want the therapist to talk about—something she does not want shared with her parents. Although I never *promise* not to tell the parents something a girl wants withheld (I only promise to *try* not to), I have almost never found it necessary to share a girl's secret. If the therapist promises not to tell her parents things she wishes to keep secret, the adolescent may be tempted to test the promise, which can put the therapist in a very difficult position. Of course, there are those rare occasions when, in order to stop an adolescent from behaving self-destructively, it really is necessary to tell her parents what she plans to do.

Often an adolescent girl will ask the therapist not to reveal that she has been sexually active or that she has tried illegal drugs. Interestingly, however, the most frequently requested secret concerns the girl having told the therapist that she hates her parents. Even though she may have repeatedly and unambivalently said that she hated her mother or her father or both, perhaps she was just angry and did not really mean it. A girl may also want to keep it quiet that she has discussed some family secret, such as her mother being drunk all the time, or her father losing his job because he was less than honest or neglectful of his duties, or her father beating her mother when they argue after he has been drinking. Although the adolescent girl may need to talk about these family problems, she usually does not want to embarrass her parents by having them find out that she has done so.

One situation that the therapist will occasionally have to deal with is the intrusive parent (most often the mother) who calls or comes in frequently and wants to know what her daughter is saying to the therapist. Such a parent can be very annoying, but, more important, she can interfere by trying to make the therapy relationship a trio of mother, daughter, and therapist. Mother is in the way. The closeness and dependency that the daughter must have with the therapist cannot develop if the mother is always there. Perhaps such interference is the mother's conscious or unconscious intent. She may not want her daughter to overcome her problems and grow too independent; she may feel that she will be less needed, more alone, and more depressed. Or she may be jealous of the attention her daughter is receiving. Or perhaps she has always intruded in her daughter's life. The mother's attitude may have contributed to the adolescent's symptoms. The girl may find it difficult to become independent and self-reliant if her mother has always been there to solve her problems for her.

With an interfering parent, it is helpful to structure the treatment from the beginning—by insisting that parents tell their daughter every time they call or see the therapist. It is inhibiting for parents to contact the therapist too frequently if they must do so; it makes them feel uncomfortable if they have to explain to their daughter why so much contact is needed. It is important for the therapist to ask the mother (or father) *each time* whether or not the patient is aware of the call. Sometimes parents have to be reminded of the structure and to have their own behavior limited. If parents resist this structure and protest telling their daughter every time they call the therapist, they can be warned that if they do not tell her the therapist will. Their daughter must know, and they will probably feel more comfortable in the long run if the girl hears about the call from them rather than from the therapist, for it could be embarrassing to have their daughter confront them with trying to keep secrets from her. If the therapist informs the patient each time one of her parents calls, she is reminding both daughter and parents of the original structure.

Occasionally a parent will contact the therapist very often, even though the daughter is made aware of the calls. If the daughter is doing well in her therapy despite the calls and is dependent on the therapist and feels comfortable talking about herself, the therapist may elect to do nothing about the situation. If the opposite is true, however, and the mother's calls seem to be interfering, the therapist will probably have to confront the mother about her behavior. At first, this confrontation should be somewhat gentle; the therapist does not want the mother to feel so offended that she stops the therapy. Stopping her daughter from seeing the therapist is, after all, the ultimate in interference.

When confronting the mother with the fact that she calls so often, the therapist can simply ask why she feels it is necessary. Sometimes a mother will say that she doesn't know whether or not her daughter is telling the therapist what is really happening. Basically, this probably means that she fears her daughter is not telling *her* side of the story. In this case, some reassurance from the therapist might well be in order. The parent and her daughter may have quarreled a great deal prior to deciding on psychotherapy; thus, it may be difficult for a mother to feel that the therapist is not against her and on the daughter's side, especially if the therapy appears to be progressing well and the girl has developed a strong dependency on the therapist. Finding out that the therapist is *not* against her can help her stop interfering.

Sometimes the mother will say that she feels left out, that she is not a part of the therapy. On such an occasion, she can be reminded that she is probably right, that she *is* left out in some ways, but that this usually happens when a child grows up. She can be asked if she needs time to get used to the fact that her daughter is growing up and does not confide in her as often now. Or she can be asked if she wants psychotherapy for herself. Does she need someone to talk with? Although the mother may not want a referral the first time she is confronted with her anxiety, she may eventually ask for one if she sees that her daughter's separation is too painful a process for her. Referring a parent for psychotherapy after such groundwork has been laid, and the problem somewhat identified, is much more palatable for a parent than simply announcing, as so many therapists do at the outset of a girl's treatment, that the parent also needs therapy. With no further explanation, the announcement implies criticism of the parent for having erred and thereby for having caused the girl's problems. If psychotherapy is recommended after the parent has had a part in the decision-making process, it is likely that both the parent and the teenage patient will be helped more effectively.

A good way to start the treatment of an adolescent girl is to ask both the adolescent and her parents to come in for an initial conference. Even when the parents are no longer living together, both are sometimes willing to attend at least one joint interview. Such a conference gives the therapist an opportunity to see how the parents interact with each other and with their daughter. Although one usually hears two views of the girl's problem—the parents' and the girl's—when the parents are not in accord, three differing views may be offered. The parents also have an opportunity to see what the therapist is like and whether the therapist seems to be blaming them. A joint conference suggests to the parents that the therapist *does* want and does value their opinions. In itself, this opportunity can reduce the amount of anxiety the parents have about sending their daughter for psychotherapy. Sometimes, the therapist may find that he or she is acting more like a traffic director than a therapist. There may be so much anger and the family may be so verbal that the therapist will have to insist that everyone be quiet and listen while another family member talks. But, even if such activity is necessary, the implied message is the same. The therapist is communicating that the parents have something important to say and that the therapy will not be an attack against them.

A joint interview for the first session is often very useful in future conversations with the adolescent girl. When asked to talk about her demeaning or disruptive behavior or about how anxious or depressed she seems to be, a girl will frequently say that this is not a problem, or that this is no longer true. She is not lying; she is using denial. She may be so embarrassed about the behavior or so pained by the anxiety or depression that she *hopes* it is no longer a problem. She *wants* things to be better by tomorrow. And if she really *believes* they will be, then, of course, there *is* no longer a problem. Such denial can be troublesome and time-consuming. But if she has participated in a discussion about the problems with both her parents and her therapist at the first interview, the adolescent will probably use denial less.

Parents sometimes bring their daughter for psychotherapy because they feel unable to handle her problematic behavior. They will complain that although they consider her behavior intolerable there is nothing they can do to stop it. They will claim that they have tried everything but that nothing works. They feel impotent and frustrated in their inability to get their daughter to behave in an acceptable manner. The case of Jan demonstrates such frustration on the part of parents.

Jan was thirteen years old, a middle child with a sister one year older and a brother three years younger. Her parents reported that Jan had always been somewhat difficult. She seemed to demand more of their attention than the others. Yet, at times, she could be extremely helpful and kind and would go out of her way to do nice things for her parents. In the past several months, Jan's demanding behavior increased to an intolerable level and she seemed to have no concern for anyone else in the family. If she could not get her way, she would yell and scream and upset everyone. If she wanted some new clothing and was told that she would have to wait her turn or that she must learn to share in the family budget, Jan would throw a tantrum. Her parents tried to tell her about sharing and waiting and about the family finances, but their "little talks" seemed to fall on deaf ears. Reasoning with her helped not at all. Jan stopped doing her chores, and she was not motivated to do her share even when her allowance was discontinued for two weeks. If Jan wanted a clean top to wear with her dirty jeans and the laundry was not yet done, she would yell at her mother and then sneak into her sister's room to take one of her sister's tops. Jan came home from school each day and dropped her books and clothes on the way to the television set, where she just sat and ate. A school counselor remarked in a parent conference that Jan seemed depressed; she was so less involved with school than before. Her parents had not noted this, but they decided that something must be wrong and brought Jan to the psychotherapist.

Jan started weekly sessions and was beginning to confide in her therapist. She talked about such things as not having friends at school and feeling left out. She said that in grade school she had had many more friends than her sister. Although she said she was popular in grade school, her description of popularity sounded as if it meant getting the other girls to do what she wanted them to. Jan talked about her jealousy of her sister, who now had so many friends, and of her brother, who seemed to excell in everything. She said her father was always worried about her brother, even though he did well, because he was the only boy in the family and was small for his age. Jan was talking about herself quite well for a thirteen-year-old.

Jan's parents asked for a conference to discuss their daughter's behavior and their inability to handle her. Jan was asked how she felt about such a conference. Jan said, "Go ahead and see them if you want. They are just going to come and complain about me some more." It really didn't seem to matter to Jan that her parents wanted to talk to her therapist. In the conference, her parents complained about her very irritating behavior and about having tried so many things to change it. They felt that it was imperative that something be done since the whole family was becoming upset, yet they felt that there was nothing *they* could do.

The therapist told Jan's parents that since the girl was so dependent on them for so many things they were definitely in a position of power or influence over her. They could, indeed, get her to change her behavior if they really insisted. They could withdraw all money for clothes, all rides to the shopping center, all lunch money, all the things they were doing for her if she refused to help around the house. The parents protested that such a tactic wouldn't work, but finally the father agreed that perhaps it might. By taking everything away from Jan, every privilege, they could get her to do her chores. He added that she would not do them promptly, that she would probably grumble all the while, and that she would most likely run the vacuun cleaner in the evening while they were watching television. The therapist said they must understand that although they could get Jan to do her chores they could not get her to *like* doing them. They were advised to go home, insist that Jan do her share of the work, and return in two weeks to report the results. They were cautioned not to expect a total personality change in that short time and were reminded that Jan did not have to like doing chores; she simply *must* do them.

Two weeks later, Jan's parents reported that their daughter was indeed doing her chores. She did not like to do them, but she was becoming less overtly angry about the work than she had been the first two days. However, Jan's parents said they were still distressed. What they had really wanted was for Jan to again be part of the family. They wanted her to like them and to show them she did as she had in the past — to do her chores because she *wanted* to do her share for the family.

Jan's parents were told that Jan was depressed, absorbed in her own problems, and also growing up; they should expect a certain distance between them and Jan which had not existed in the past and which would probably continue until Jan was less depressed. Expressed in this way, they could accept Jan's attitude more readily. They were advised to continue to insist that Jan do her share of the chores, that it would be helpful for her. They agreed.

Jan's depression soon eased. When she was less depressed and more outgoing, the girls in her class became more interested in her again. She came to see, with the aid of her therapy, that if she wanted friends she had to be more giving and less demanding. She needed to do some of the things the other girls wanted to do; she could not always have her own way. Jan started bringing some friends home, and her mother was delighted and helped entertain them. She was glad to be sharing with her daughter again, and Jan's depression eased even more.

Jan's parents were not as impotent as they had thought they were in getting Jan to do what they expected. In this case, the parent conferences were very valuable. The parents discovered what they really wanted from their daughter and learned that it was impossible for Jan to give them the attention and closeness they wished for at this time. When Jan's parents recognized that their daughter's refusal to do her chores was a symptom of her depression and not a rejection of them, they were ready to follow the therapist's advice. They were able to insist that Jan do her share since the therapist was convinced such insistence would help. Jan felt better about herself when she was not allowed to selfishly avoid her chores.

As with so many younger adolescents, Jan did not seem especially concerned about her parents' and therapist's conferences. She knew what her parents wanted to discuss—as do so many girls. They themselves have heard their parents' complaints many times before.

Another topic that parents frequently want to discuss with a psychotherapist is what they perceive as their child's underachievement in school or a seeming rejection of the family's cultural value of achievement. Children who are underachieving are frequently depressed and can be helped with psychotherapy, but the therapy is much more likely to succeed if parents participate in the treatment. Conferences with the parents are necessary to help them understand what they themselves can no *in the present*—not what they could have done better in the past. Consider the case of Cindy, a fifteen-year-old girl who was her father's favorite. Cindy had just received the first six-weeks progress report for her sophomore year of high school; her grades were very poor, and her parents were alarmed. Since Cindy had also done poorly in her freshman year, it was becoming apparent to her parents that her grades were not likely to improve unless there was some intervention.

Cindy's parents were both working professionals. Cindy's only sibling, a sister, was away at college and doing well. The family knew the therapist, who had treated Cindy's sister in psychotherapy for two years, terminating the year before. The parents said that since the therapist had treated the older girl, and knew the family well, there was no need to look for another therapist.

Cindy's sister had been a very anxious child and an even more anxious adolescent. She struggled to obtain good grades in school and worked hard to find a large circle of friends, which had been difficult for her. Since she was determined to succeed in everything she did, she suffered much anxiety and many disappointments. She had demanded much of her parents' attention, and she had received it. Cindy, in contrast, was "easy" to raise. She was always pleasant, well liked by peers and adults, had always seemed content, and demanded little of her parents' energies. In the midst of the parents' efforts to help their older daughter, Cindy was overlooked.

Cindy was seen twice and then the parents came in for a conference with the therapist. Cindy turned out to be the pleasant, easy-going child that her mother had described on the telephone. She related to the therapist easily but preferred to talk about music and her guitar lessons rather than her low grades. She appeared to be an intelligent child who knew much about the world, having read extensively on her own in ecology, politics, and photography, as well as in her current interest, music. Cindy stated that she was not concerned about her grades even though her parents were; she did not think grades in school had much to do with a real education. She also said that she was determined to make her future career with her music, to be a performer, and that she had little need for a formal education. Although she professed great interest in playing the guitar and singing, she missed many of her lessons and had difficulty getting herself to practice; thus she felt her progress was very slow. In fact, she was thinking about giving up trying to read music and just play by ear.

Cindy's parents came in for their conference, upset over her low grades. They felt that since everyone else in the family had a college education Cindy might feel less worthy, might have a poor self-image, if she did not. And if her grades did not improve, she would not have the option of going to college. "What has happened to our little girl who never gave us any problems?" they wondered.

The therapist could have explored with the parents why the mother's favorite child, the one she had identified with, had struggled so hard to achieve, while the father's favorite, Cindy, did not. Or the therapist could have explored the reasons for the relative neglect of the second child compared to the attention the eldest had received. Or the therapist could have brought up the father's passivity compared to the mother's aggressiveness. But it seemed more timely to discuss what the parents could *now* do, not to go into the past or examine the possibility of parental psychopathology. The therapist asked the parents if they had ever told Cindy directly that they expected her to get good grades. They had not. But, they asked, why was the older girl so competitive for grades and did her best to achieve academically and socially when they had never told her to compete and achieve? It was explained that some children seem to intuitively pick the family's cultural values, which other children need explicit messages from their parents. They were told that they must give Cindy a clear and unambivalent message that they expected her to achieve academically.

A joint interview with the girl, her parents, and the therapist was arranged so that the parents could let Cindy know what they expected of her and why. But the parents found it difficult to tell their daughter that they expected her to be competitive for grades. Although they wanted their children to achieve, they wanted it to seem that it was their children's desire to do so. They did not like to think of themselves as demanding or authoritarian parents. After that conference, appointments were set up once a week, with Cindy coming one week and her parents the next. Everyone was agreeable to this arrangement.

In her hours with the therapist, Cindy continued to talk about her interest in music and about a small musical group she and some friends were forming. She also talked about school, saying that she had never really studied very hard. In grade school she had done well, but she felt that grade school teachers took the responsibility for motivating a student and making the work interesting. In contrast, high school teachers just presented the material and left it up to the student to motivate herself and study on her own. She found it difficult to make herself study; she lost interest easily.

In conferences with Cindy's parents, the therapist said that the parents must see to it that Cindy did her homework each night or at least see to it that she sat at her desk with the work in front of her. They were told that they should not let her go out on school nights and not let her go to concerts on weekends, no matter who was performing, unless she was caught up in her work. They must insist that she study. Although they hated this role of policing their daughter, they agreed to be strict; the therapist convinced them that they had to be in order to give Cindy a clear message as to what they expected of her.

In her sessions, Cindy started wondering about the music group she and her friends were forming. The others seemed to have so little initiative; they didn't really practice and played poorly. Her own guitar playing, however, was improving. She decided to join another group whose members were better performers and who played at a few dances and parties. Her schoolwork was also improving, but she complained a bit about her parents watching her so closely. She started talking about college, saying now that she had always intended to go to college since it was hard to amount to anything in this world without a college education.

Cindy's parents by now were becoming weary of their task and asked the therapist if they really had to be so strict. Was the therapist sure that this was the right thing to do? The therapist said that she was sure and that they must continue. They did.

After a while Cindy discovered that her ability to discipline herself to study varied. If she worked regularly every night, she could keep up the pace. If there was an interruption in school, such as a long weekend or a vacation, she would let down and have trouble getting back in the routine. She noticed this because she had examinations coming up and she had not done much work since the Christmas holiday. She was unable to make herself study, and she was worried. She had never expressed concern about her grades before. Her therapist asked her if she really wanted to get back into her study routine and if she was willing to request help from her parents. Cindy said she wanted help, but she knew if she did ask for it that her father would check up on her every fifteen minutes and her mother would want to know about every project and wonder just how well she was doing. Still, Cindy decided that she wanted to ask her parents for help. A conference was held later that same day. Her parents asked what Cindy wanted them to do, and she said that she wanted her father to help her with her math and that she wanted both of them to watch her closely and make sure that she was working. They did just that. When they got home, her father went immediately to Cindy's bedroom and took the radio out. He or his wife looked in on Cindy every fifteen minutes to see if she were studying, and they stayed up late with her the next few nights to be sure she got her work done. Cindy was now motivated to do well and had incorporated the values of achieving and competing to such an extent that she claimed these had been her values and goals all along. She was even willing to ask her parents to help her achieve her goals.

Cindy had more work to do in her therapy, but the goal of the first phase had been accomplished; she had begun to achieve in school. She had not really been aware that her parents felt she was as capable as her sister. It is also possible that she needed attention from her parents and unconsciously wanted them to suffer as revenge for not having been more attentive earlier. Her parents did suffer and anguish some, while they also gave her attention. It was hard for them to insist that she achieve and then police her, but they did it. Cindy's needs for attention and making her parents suffer were met constructively by having the parents insist that she study.

As this case illustrates, a great deal of direct advice can be given to the parents of the adolescent girl. The parents listened to the therapist and tried hard to follow the advice they received. Past errors or oversights on the part of the parents in raising their daughters were hardly mentioned. The emphasis was clearly on the here and now. It is also interesting that the girl never objected to her therapist seeing the parents every other week. She seemed quite comfortable with her therapist despite these conferences.

Thirteen-year-old Vicki came to her first therapy session accompanied by her mother, stepfather, and ten-year-old brother. The family decided on a joint appointment because they said they weren't sure who had the problem. Only the ten-year-old boy knew that *he* could not be the problem. The others felt that they might be responsible for the tension in the home, but the mother and stepfather pretty much agreed that Vicki was very difficult to live with at this time and that the tension might be centered around her.

The mother and stepfather had married three years ago, and the mother had continued working. She was pleased that she had been able to support herself and her two children for the three years between her first and second marriages. She had risen to manager of the shoe department in a large store and felt that her success was a great achievement; she did not wish to give up her work. The stepfather was also employed in sales, but he also did much of the housework, all the grocery shopping, and all the cooking since his wife hated to cook. The mother decorated the house and bought the clothes. Although the stepfather was satisfied with this arrangement, he felt the children must help by doing daily chores. They were required to empty the dishwasher, take the garbage out, and vacuum the living room once weekly, in addition to keeping their rooms clean. Both mother and stepfather agreed that these were reasonable duties for the children. Right after school every day, the ten-year-old boy immediately did his chores. Vicki usually did not do hers at all.

Vicki's stepfather and brother complained about Vicki's attitude as well as her refusal to do chores. She was haughty and aloof and expected things to be given to her and done for her, and she never seemed appreciative even when she got what she wanted. Her stepfather frequently went out of town on business and usually brought back gifts for the children. Vicki would not even say thank you. Two weeks earlier, he had bought Vicki an expensive coat she wanted, and after she showed no appreciation and did not thank him, he became very angry with her. He had refused to talk to her since, and the family tension had become unbearable. Although the stepfather felt Vicki was the cause of the tension, he was unsure since his wife said he was too demanding. Another complication was that both the children and the stepfather were irritated because of the way the mother spoiled her two dogs. All three felt the dogs got too much of her attention and that they, in turn, were neglected. The family agreed to the following psychotherapy arrangement: Vicki was to be seen by the therapist every other week by herself, and on the alternate weeks various other family members could be seen with or without Vicki.

In her sessions, Vicki complained mostly about her mother. She said that her mother expected her to be a genius who could do her homework without any difficulty. Although she had been an excellent student in grade school, she said it was because she had studied and the other students had not. In high school, however, more students did their homework and studied for tests, and thus it was not now as easy for her to excel. Vicki was tired of her mother talking about her being a genius and a superior human being.

The stepfather, in a session by himself, said that he had been very unhappy after his first divorce. He had missed family life and seeing his children grow up. Now he liked having a family again and was willing to do a lot to get along with his wife and stepchildren. He did not mind doing the cooking and grocery shopping; it made him feel part of the family. He enjoyed buying his wife and children gifts, but the recent incident was more abuse than he was willing to accept. He had purchased the expensive coat that Vicki had longed for and had received no appreciation, no "thank you." Even he could not stand her attitude any longer.

Vicki was still complaining of her mother. She talked about her mother's excessive drinking, saying that her moods were unpredictable when she drank. She could be happy and affectionate, too much so, and then could suddenly change and become angry with Vicki or anyone about her.

When the mother came in to see the psychotherapist alone, she was quite uncomfortable. She said that she expected to get all the blame for the tensions at home and to be criticized for spoiling her dogs. She acknowledged that she treated the dogs better than she treated anyone in the family. Vicki's mother seemed to anticipate that she would be blamed for the problems at home.

She defensively said that everyone blamed her, and she offered her indulgence with the dogs as the reason, hoping no one would look further to find her at fault for other things. The psychotherapist said it was of little practical value to try to pinpoint one person in the family who was the most to blame. Why not find out who could do something to ease the tensions?

Somewhat reassured, the mother went on to say that she never really liked children; she had decided to have children because all her friends were. Since her philosophy was always "anything you can do, I can do better," she was going to have better children than her friends. When Vicki was very young, she spent many hours teaching her to talk, to count, and eventually to print her name. Vicki could read before she went to school. The mother knew that Vicki was a superior human being. In grade school, Vicki's teachers often remarked that Vicki did her work well but that she seemed to have an inflated opinion of herself. The mother hastened to add that she always told these teachers that if a human being is superior it can be expected that the person will have a superior attitude.

On alternate weeks, Vicki now talked about a friend whom her mother would not allow her to see. Her mother felt that the friend's family was beneath them socially and said Vicki must not see the girl again. Vicki had been caught leaving the house at night, after her parents were asleep, to visit this friend. She liked the girl. She did not feel that her mother should choose her friends. She was so lonely. Now her mother was thinking of moving to a new and larger house, but a house away from her friend's. If her mother bought this new house, then Vicki would have to go to a new school, and she would never see her friend.

The mother, in an individual session with the therapist, talked about feeling the need to make some decision. Her husband was angry and said that he wanted more respect from Vicki, that he wanted Vicki to talk to him and appreciate the things he was doing for her. He seemed so insistent. The mother was thinking of a divorce, but she realized how helpful her husband was in seeing to it that the children weren't getting into all the kinds of trouble possible in these days. She feared she could not keep her children safe from such dangers without her husband's help. Yet, she could not stand to have anyone tell her how to raise her children, nor could she tolerate requiring that Vicki be nice to her stepfather. She described herself as the sort of person who knew how to get ahead; she could make herself be nice to people but preferred to remain aloof and demanding. Similarly, she liked to see Vicki remain aloof and not have to be nice to anyone unless she wanted to be. This was the mother's secret and the reason she feared being confronted and accused—not because she spoiled her dogs. After the therapist had reassured her that searching for someone to blame would be of little help, the mother could then talk about her behavior, which she feared was at the root of the problems.

The therapist resisted accusing Vicki's mother of encouraging Vicki's aloofness and demanding attitude but instead offered the following suggestions. The therapist pointed out that the woman apparently knew how to handle people—knew when she had to be nice and when she could act as she wished. Apparently, her daughter had not yet learned this lesson; Vicki could only be demanding and regal. The girl should be told to try to get along with her stepfather. This would ease the tensions in the family, but it would also be good for Vicki to realize that it was sometimes necessary to adjust to others and be nice to them. Mother agreed that Vicki needed to learn to act this way if she was to get anywhere in the world. Her only misgiving was that she hated to see Vicki "practice" on her stepfather. When the therapist pointed out that the stepfather was the only logical person right now, the mother agreed to tell Vicki to try to be nice to him.

At her next session with the therapist, Vicki reported that she and her stepfather were getting along just fine. She did not know why; perhaps he came home in a good mood. At any rate, they were talking to each other again, and she was trying to be appreciative and was doing her chores—at least most of them.

The psychotherapist saw Vicki and her family for a few more sessions, but no real therapeutic relationships were established. The problem was ameliorated so that the whole family was getting along better, and that was why they had come to the therapist in the first place. Vicki underwent no real personality change but was learning to be nice to someone. The mother had been persuaded to insist that Vicki behave more appropriately.

Several points are demonstrated by this brief encounter with a psychotherapist. The adolescent girl did alter her behavior when her mother wanted or allowed her to do so. Conferences with the mother were important. The woman expected to be blamed for her mishandling of the family yet was encouraged to look to the present instead of to the past. When the mother learned that she was not expected to account for her past behavior, she proceeded to talk fairly comfortably about the present situation. Of particular interest in this case was the directness with which the mother and stepfather could talk to the therapist. This atmosphere of openness was created by keeping the parents thinking and talking about the present and not the past.

Sometimes parents react too strongly to the disruptive behavior of their teenage daughter. The daughter's behavior may be distressing and may be a call for help, but overreaction by parents can make the situation worse. It can cause the adolescent to feel that she really is very different or very bad or very sick. Advising such parents about handling their daughter is imperative so that they do not cause her to develop a poor self-image. The case of Pat, involving overly distressed parents, is an example of how the therapist can advise such parents.

Pat, fifteen years old, was referred for psychotherapy by a probation officer whom her parents contacted when they felt they could no longer handle their daughter. The probation officer felt that psychological treatment seemed more appropriate than involving the probation department.

Pat's parents were frightened by her behavior. They had discovered one night that their daughter climbed out a window to meet a girlfriend. The girls had drunk some combination of alcoholic beverages that Pat's friend took from her parents' home. They had wandered the streets and strung toilet paper over the homes of two boys from school. This was not the first such incident; Pat had done the same thing a year earlier and also two months earlier, but each time with a different girl. This was not the height of the football season when a group of students sometimes get together to pull such pranks. There was no group involved, just one lonely teenage girl seeking to entertain one other girl in her efforts to find a friend. The situation was a bit unusual, and Pat was indicating her need for help. Her parents described

Pat as having much trouble finding and keeping friends, so they were not surprised that she was with a different girl each time.

Pat's family was intact. There were three daughters, one — a year older than Pat — was small, attractive, a cheerleader, and very popular with both boys and girls from her school. She was a girl who made her parents proud. The youngest daughter was eight years old and seemed to be an average child who caused no problems. Pat frequently picked on her younger sister, mercilessly, until her younger sister cried and the parents would have to intervene. The mother was not employed outside the home. The father had held the same job for twenty years, making reservations and selling tickets for an airline. The family led a stable and very predictable life. They often saw their relatives and celebrated all holidays with them. Every Easter, for example, Pat's family entertained all the relatives; almost ritualistically, they would turn on the heat in their swimming pool and prepare the same dinner menu. Neither the mother nor the father had done any acting out as adolescents, and neither had their siblings. Everyone in the family seemed to have grown up normally; they remained close to their parents and siblings, and each found a local job and a spouse who fit into the family pattern. Pat's older sister's adolescence was not problematic. Indeed, Pat's parents were very perplexed about why they were having problems with Pat. They were angry with her and told her that she was bad and must change.

Pat found the therapy situation very difficult and never became completely comfortable. She continued to see her "need" for psychotherapy as yet another way in which she was different from the rest of her family. She did see the therapist for six months, however, as she had promised the probation officer. Actually, she came for sessions exactly six months.

It became clear that Pat was having a lot of difficulty establishing an identity for herself within her family. When she behaved differently or had differing interests from her parents and her older sister, her parents were distressed. They really were very suspicious of anything out of the ordinary. Yet if Pat tried to do some of the things her sister did, such as trying to become a cheerleader, her mother would tell Pat that she was just trying to copy her sister again. She would remind Pat that she "always did that."

Shortly after therapy started, Pat became very interested in an active church group near her home. This interest really distressed her parents, and they came to talk with the therapist. The youth group was in a Protestant church other than the one the family belonged to, but the parents acknowledged that their church's youth group was not very active. The therapist advised them to visit the new church, talk to the youth group leader, and find out for themselves whether or not this might be a wholesome group for their daughter. They did so, and reported that the group seemed fine and that they had no objections to their daughter attending the meetings and activities. Pat, with the aid of the therapist, had now found something that she could do that was different but still acceptable.

In another conference, the parents were told that Pat's leaving the house at night was an indication she was having problems and was asking for something but that their alarm seemed a bit excessive. The therapist also explained that they seemed totally unaware of the problems many parents face when raising their adolescents. Since their first daughter had not given them trouble, they were probably unrealistic in expecting that their other two daughters be perfect. They were asked to join a Parents' Effectiveness Training Group that met in a local hospital once a week so that they could learn more about the problems facing teenagers and their parents. They were told that they would not have to talk about their problems with Pat unless they wanted to.

The Parents' Effectiveness Groups were open "rap" sessions to which all local parents were invited. Parents could attend once or regularly, as they wished. Although organized by a hospital social worker, the groups were led by parents and were designed to be educational and not group therapy. But the parents did discuss their problems raising their children and learned from each other. Occasionally, speakers were invited, depending on the group's preference.

There are many possible explanations for the tensions between Pat and her parents. Perhaps they were the naive family they seemed, and thus Pat's deviation from the family norms really could have been frightening. Perhaps Pat's acting out started because of her inability to tolerate living in the shadow of her sister. Perhaps the mother, since she was the eldest in *her* family, favored her older daughter and did not enjoy seeing Pat approach the achievements of the older girl; the mother might have been reliving her own childhood. Perhaps Pat's birth, so soon after her sister's, distressed the mother and she could never feel close to this second child. To attempt to determine if any psychopathology existed within this family seemed quite unwise. The family was psychologically unsophisticated and too easily frightened by psychological searching; they might have abandoned their efforts in Pat's behalf if such things were discussed. The referral to the parent discussion group sufficed to help them see that their daughter's behavior was not nearly as deviant as they had thought.

The parents became much less critical of Pat, and the girl attempted to please them more, but she continued to find activities, as well as an identity for herself, that were a bit different. Since the psychotherapy lasted only six months, the therapist did not have an opportunity to help Pat complete her identity struggle, but the groundwork was laid for Pat to find her own identity without being condemned by her parents.

If the therapist notices that there is some problem in the way the girl's parents are handling her, the therapist can ask the parents to come in for a conference. Conferences do not have to be initiated by the parents. The parents can be confronted in a direct, but supportive, manner *if* the emphasis is on their current parenting and not on past deficiencies. Most parents respond positively to direct suggestions. If not, they will usually explain why they cannot or will not follow certain advice with the same directness the therapist uses. An example of this direct way of dealing with parents can be seen in the case of Betsy, a ten-year-old girl who had been in psychotherapy for about two years.

Betsy was diagnosed as a borderline schizophrenic child who also had many learning problems. She had difficulty communicating with people and understanding the communication and behavior of others. Her thinking was very concrete. As an infant, and following the divorce of her parents, Betsy suffered deprivation and even malnutrition at the hands of her mother. Her mother committed suicide not too long after the divorce and the three children were placed with their father, who soon remarried. Betsy had no memory of her natural mother.

At the beginning of her treatment, Betsy spent her play therapy hours running from one activity to another; her attention span was about two minutes. She had to try everything for fear of missing something. She ravenously sought all activities and toys but could not really play. She could not talk about her feelings and seemed unaware of what was going on around her.

By the end of a year and a half of therapy, Betsy was able to tell the therapist if she was upset. The therapist would then attempt to figure out what was happening and try to explain the situation to her. For example, one day Betsy came in crying, saying that one of the boys at school had said she was fat. In reality, Betsy was extremely thin. The therapist called Betsy's teacher and learned that the boy was himself rather obese. The therapist then told Betsy that she was not fat at all, but that the boy was fat and that it probably bothered him. That was why he told her *she* was fat. Betsy appreciated the explanation and decided that if it bothered the boy so much that he was fat, she would let him call her fat. Maybe that would make him feel better. But she was not going to be upset any more.

Another time, Betsy had been teased by two children in her class. The therapist, knowing that the school was recently integrated, asked Betsy if there were any troubles in her class between the black children and the white children. Betsy thought about that question a while and then said there were no black children in her class. She added that there were no white children in her class either. She said, "We have some tan children, and some brown ones, and some who are sort of peach-colored." Betsy obviously had difficulty conceptualizing things as most people do and consequently found it difficult to communicate because of this. Her viewpoint was very refreshing but unlike others' conceptualizations.

At one point, Betsy started to repeatedly play with the dolls in her sessions, and this behavior continued for several weeks. She would undress the dolls and be sure that the therapist noticed that all were naked. It seemed that she was trying to communicate something, so the therapist asked the father to come in for a conference. The father was told that Betsy's play had changed recently and that it was repetitious and she seemed to be trying to say something. He was told about the nude dolls and asked about nudity in the home. He said that he and his wife were not in the habit of running around nude. After thinking about it a while, he said that he gave Betsy a bath every night and then put her to bed. His wife worked and was tired in the evenings so he wanted to help; and, at any rate, he liked doing so. The therapist suggested that it might be best if he stopped giving Betsy her bath. His wife could do so, or Betsy could bathe alone. Father looked sad as he said, "But that's my little girl." He agreed to stop the baths, but he asked why Betsy had never seemed embarrassed or told him in any way that it bothered her. He was reminded that Betsy could not communicate very well. Betsy's play with the nude dolls was never repeated.

The therapist could have explored the father's incestuous interests in his daughter, but a great many fathers seem to have such feelings to some extent. This father may have been no different from most. Telling him directly what to do, and what *not* to do, was helpful and he responded to the suggestion. Besides, he himself was in therapy with another therapist, and if his interests in his daughter were a problem, he had an opportunity to discuss these feelings elsewhere. Dealing with this father very directly, in a noncritical manner that did not dwell on his past parenting, was effective in Betsy's case.

Even when their daughter is not in psychotherapy, parents will occasionally seek advice as to how they might best handle some crisis situation. In the following case, Jackie's parents wanted advice, and they received it. They went to a psychotherapist on the recommendation of a probation officer, who talked with them after Jackie, fifteen years old, had run away from home for the third time in the past five weeks. This last time she was away two days and nights. Up until Jackie's first runaway, her parents had noted no particular problem with their daughter. She attended a parochial school, where she did fairly well. She had a few friends at school but was not socially active otherwise. Most of the time, she seemed to prefer the company of her three younger siblings. Prior to psychotherapy, Jackie was taken to a gynecologist and found to be pregnant; arrangements had already been made for an abortion that both Jackie and her parents wanted. In the two one-hour sessions, Jackie related to the therapist as if she were somewhat younger than she was and deferred to her parents. She was not able to express herself well or solve her own problems. After bringing Jackie in twice, the parents saw the therapist several times and clearly wanted advice on how to handle the present crisis. They were not interested in psychotherapy for Jackie herself.

Jackie's parents became alarmed when they found they could not stop Jackie seeing the young man who got her pregnant. And now, the young man had just died from an overdose of barbiturates. Joe had been a member of a motorcycle gang and used drugs freely. Because of his sudden death, the gang was starting to idealize Joe; the members contacted Jackie, telling her not to have the abortion since she would be killing Joe's baby. Jackie still wanted the abortion, but she also wanted to spend time with Joe's friends. Jackie told the therapist that she had not been in love with Joe and that she had known him just the five weeks, but she seemed to enjoy the gang's attention for being the girl who was carrying the baby of their dead friend.

Joe's friends were planning a big funeral. Jackie made it quite clear to her parents and the therapist that she intended to run away or do whatever was necessary to attend that funeral. She said that there was no way her parents could watch her every minute and she was going to get away. Psychotherapy for Jackie was recommended on the basis that Jackie's behavior needed to be understood better if further difficulties were to be prevented. The parents refused. They described themselves as a seclusive family who could not tolerate any intrusion other than what was absolutely necessary.

Jackie's parents were told that it would be a mistake to try to stop Jackie from attending the funeral. They had already assumed she would get there one way or another. The therapist then said that if she went alone, Jackie would undoubtedly be the center of attraction and would enjoy it. As everyone sat around talking about Joe and Joe's baby, Jackie might feel even greater affinity with the group and develop the identity of being one of them. Although Jackie at this point saw herself as a girl who had an escapade with a motorcycle gang member over her summer vacation, she did not see herself as a member of a motorcycle group; she had not as yet developed such an identity. Yet it could happen if she became more involved with the gang members at the funeral.

The father understood the situation and was concerned. He was asked if he were willing to attend the funeral with Jackie and see to it that she did not go to the party afterward. He was obviously distressed at this idea but said he could do so if necessary. After the funeral, the father talked to the therapist and said he was revolted and humiliated at the experience but had tried not to express his feelings. He wondered how people could dress and act that way at a funeral. It apparently was such a bizarre event that Jackie told her father that she, too, was upset by it all. Jackie, in seeing this dramatic scene with her father at her side, had an opportunity to observe the contrast between one life-style and another. She had gone to the services dressed like a young lady who was attending a funeral. She accepted this as her cultural norm or her identity. Yet, there were the others, Joe's friends, dressed in their "costumes." She went home right after the services, changed her clothes, and played with her siblings like a little girl. They all went fishing at a small pond near home, with her parents watching in the background.

The father was about to leave town on business, and the therapist advised him to take Jackie along. She was eager to go. He was told that this would take Jackie away from the gang and that, after a week or so, she would probably be "old news" and thus no longer of much interest to Joe's friends. The father was also advised that when the two of them were away he should let Jackie talk about Joe if she wished; he should not try to stop her or remind her that he considered Joe a bad person. He was told that when people have a loss, they need to mourn and talk about it to someone; he had the choice of letting Jackie talk to him or of forcing her to go to Joe's friends to talk. He seemed to understand and agreed to follow the advice.

Two weeks later, the father contacted the therapist and said the trip had gone well and that Jackie did talk about Joe a few times. He had just listened when she recalled some of the good things about Joe, such as his love of animals and his kindness. He had wanted to tell Jackie that Joe was no good but remembered that he had been instructed by the therapist not to do so.

When the summer was over, Jackie returned to school almost as if nothing had happened. She did not run away again and related to her family as before. The parents kept in touch with the therapist as they were instructed to, but they never could be persuaded to let Jackie come to psychotherapy. The problem was over, and they did not want to learn why it had happened and did not feel Jackie needed to learn either. Yet they always expressed gratitude for the therapist's advice and felt it had been helpful.

The paramount reason for the advice given to the parents in this case was the girl's identity. Although she did not appear to see herself as a member of the motorcycle group subculture, Jackie could have developed such an identity because of the pregnancy and the romantic mystique that can occur in such a situation. As an immature teenager, she did not yet have a fixed identity; it could be altered. A question of values was involved. The therapist actively made moves and gave suggestions that would help prevent Jackie from developing the identity of a gang member; the girl was not left to flounder and perhaps choose an identity inappropriate for her. The identity of a member of a motorcycle gang is not a very satisfying one. Also, since Jackie let it be known that she was thinking about running away and joining the group in the first session with the therapist, she must have been asking for help to stop her doing so. If she had not wanted someone to stop her, she could have kept her thoughts secret.

While this case is a somewhat unusual situation, since the family came to a psychotherapist and yet refused therapy, the principle of giving direct advice is illustrated. The parents were not criticized for their parenting. They wanted advice, received it, and followed it to the best of their ability.

The cases reported in this chapter demonstrate that conferences with the parents of an adolescent girl in therapy can be extremely helpful and, in many instances, essential for successful treatment.

Parent-therapist conferences at the outset of treatment have several advantages compared to recommending that the parents seek therapy for themselves. If the parents themselves start in psychotherapy, the girl's therapist does not know whether or not they will first work on their relationship with their daughter. They may have other things they wish to talk about in the beginning of their own therapy sessions. Also, since the goal of psychotherapy with adults is usually to produce insight, the parents' therapist might not feel as free to give direct advice as the girl's therapist talking to them in a parent conference. Further, many parents will refuse or resist any psychotherapy for themselves, feeling that it is their daughter who is having the problems. But they probably will not refuse to come to confer with their daughter's psychotherapist, and this, of course, is the ultimate advantage.

Parent conferences can be held by the therapist treating the adolescent girl or by another mental health professional. Generally, an adolescent patient does not seem upset when her therapist also sees her parents. A good therapeutic relationship can be maintained with the girl despite such conferences. In these conferences, the therapist does not need to point out whatever psychopathology he or she sees or suspects is present. Advice to the parents should be given with emphasis on the present, the here and now. What has gone on in the past is not nearly as important as what the parents can now do to help their adolescent daughter.

EIGHT

Guidelines for
the Therapist

The philosophy of psychother-
apy with adolescent girls presented in this book rests equally on
pragmatism and an understanding of psychodynamics. In this
chapter, I review this philosophy from the viewpoint of the psychotherapist's role.

A psychotherapist working with the adolescent girl needs to
keep in mind the major developmental tasks of adolescence when
assessing the girl's problems and determining treatment goals.
The girl will have accomplished these tasks when she has achieved
some sense of separateness from her parents; recognized that she
is an individual with her own identity; and developed a sense of
mastery, a feeling that she can handle her own urges and impulses and can cope with the demands of the world. The therapist
will usually find that neurotic symptoms are maladaptive attempts to complete these developmental stages. If depressed, she

may be reacting to the futility she is experiencing, to the feeling that she will not be able to leave her parents' side. Even as her identity develops, she may react to her sense of failure in not fulfilling the expectations of her ego ideal; she may expect more of herself than she can produce. If she experiences undue anxiety, underneath she may fear losing control of her impulses or feel discomfort and fear in trying to cope with the new demands placed on her because she is now maturing. If she is acting out, she may be making an abortive attempt to deny her fear of separating from her parents or to decrease the all-too-comfortable closeness and compatability that earlier existed between her and her parents. Looking at symptoms as maladaptive and keeping in mind the developmental tasks of adolescence helps a therapist determine what moves will be helpful.

When delineating treatment goals and approaches, a psychotherapist should assess the personalities of both the adolescent girl and her parents. Perhaps the therapist will determine that one of the parents has undermined the adolescent girl's sense of self-confidence to handle new situations by having rescued her too often when she faced difficult situations in the past or by belittling her accomplishments when she did handle a situation competently. Perhaps one of her parents, fearing loss of companionship, feels the need to keep the girl dependent and tied to the family and thus fosters the dependency. Or, one of her parents may covertly condone her acting out to camouflage other family psychopathology. If the behavior of the parents appears to be causing the girl significant difficulties in completing the developmental tasks of adolescence, the psychotherapist has to determine how to deal with the parents and what advice to give them. Yet the psychotherapist must also try to determine whether or not the adolescent is blaming her parents for her own fears, anxieties, or failures; she may be trying to deny her problems or to rationalize them. If, despite obvious evidence that she herself is having difficulties, she honestly claims she feels there are no problems, she is using denial. Rationalization is a ubiquitous defense mechanism. It is easy, and frequently necessary, for a person to place the blame for lack of achievements on a boss who does not appreciate what one does, on a wife who is not supportive, on those people in an in-group who only help each other, or on the world for not yet being ready for one's ideas. When an adolescent girl uses such rationalization, she may need a defense against being overwhelmed by her inadequacies. A skillful psychotherapist, however, can reduce her rationalization a bit at a time even as he or she helps the girl deal with the world's demands more skillfully and accomplish more.

But how does the psychotherapist decide if the behavior of the parents is largely responsible for the adolescent girl's maladjustment or whether the girl is blaming them for her problems as a defense? Frequently both conditions are present at the same time and both need to be worked on for the psychotherapy to be successful. The therapist can help clarify the dilemma by assessing the girl's ability to handle the demands she faces. If the adolescent girl has effected almost no separateness from her parents and has few, if any, skills or successes and almost no friends, the psychotherapist should suspect that she may be trying to rationalize her problems, fears, or failures as she enthusiastically points to her parents' psychopathology.

Despite popular notions to the contrary, the same psychotherapist can work with both the adolescent girl and her parents. If a therapist decides to do so, he or she should explain the ground rules very carefully at the outset. The girl must be told of every conference or phone call between her parents and the therapist, preferably *before* the contact. Then, if she asks, she can be told the general content of the conversation. Both the parents and the adolescent girl should be assured that their confidences will be respected, but the therapist should not *promise* to keep everything the girl says a secret from her parents. After all, the therapist may find it vital to tell the parents something to prevent a self-destructive acting out on their daughter's part. If the therapist establishes these ground rules clearly and follows them carefully, the adolescent girl can develop the feelings of confidence and confidentiality necessary for successful psychotherapy, even though she knows that her therapist and parents sometimes confer.

The therapist should be prepared to give the parents direct advice on what they can do or stop doing in order to help their daughter. It is important for parents not to get the impression that the therapist is critical of them. Tact should always be used. It is also important for the therapist to give advice that concerns only the parents' present behavior or attitudes toward their daughter. A discussion of past inconsistencies or neglect in their parenting helps little and can even alienate them. Discussions of childrearing practices should be in the present, the here and now, and not delve into the past. If parents bring their daughter to psychotherapy willingly, out of concern for her, they are prone to seek and will attempt to follow the therapist's advice. Many are willing to forego their own needs, if they are convinced that doing so is in the best interests of their daughter. But most parents are not willing or are not able to handle the guilt and anger that is aroused by discussions of previous deficient parenting; after all, they cannot change the past.

The therapist will need to be quite active in sessions with the adolescent. Therapy with the adolescent girl does not parallel or even resemble insight-oriented psychotherapy with the neurotic, yet relatively healthy adult. When appropriate, the therapist should be supportive and sympathetic. He or she should also be active in giving advice and in suggesting how the girl can practice dealing with the demands of the world until she is able to handle those demands on her own.

One of the most important, and yet frequently underrated, tasks of the psychotherapist is to help the adolescent girl develop a sense of mastery. This sense of mastery is two phased, and the girl may lack either (or both) of the elements. She must become capable of handling her own impulses and urges, and she also needs to develop the sense of mastery or self-confidence necessary for dealing with the demands of the world.

A psychotherapist can help the adolescent girl learn to delay acting out long enough to consider its consequences. If the girl is a younger adolescent, she can be told unambivalently that she must stop acting out her impulses and urges; steps can be taken to simply stop her. If she is older and more purposeful in her actions, she can be subtly persuaded to stop and discuss her behavior. Persuasion and logical discussion are not usually, in themselves, enough to dissuade this older girl from acting out; some deterrents will probably be needed, such as a loss of privileges or the disapproval of her parents. With the younger girl, strong force with only sketchy explanations are most effective, for wordy explanations can only add fuel to the argument.

The psychotherapist stops the girl's acting out because it is overtly self-destructive or self-demeaning. The message to the girl is that the behavior is unacceptable, unsafe, or both. Although the girl will resist initially, if the psychotherapy is successful, she will identify with the therapist and incorporate his or her values as her own. She will act out less. The psychotherapist is not just trying to decide what behavior is appropriate for her but is teaching her something extremely important—to delay, to think, and to control her impulses.

The psychotherapist—by reviewing with the adolescent girl her day-to-day interactions with people, her successes and failures, and the decisions she has made or needs to make—can do a great deal to help the girl develop a sense of mastery. It is important for the disturbed adolescent girl to learn what works for her and what does not. She must come to see how others react to her attitudes and behavior, how others feel in similar situations, and how others have handled situations similar to the one she now finds herself in. Discussions of these subjects are the core of ongoing psychotherapy. In the course of such conversations, the girl will learn something about her therapist and how he or she deals with the world. Tutelage from and identification with the psychotherapist can be immensely valuable in the process of achieving mastery.

The psychotherapist should rarely interpret to either the adolescent girl or her parents the unconscious meanings of their behavior. Most families and most disturbed adolescent girls cannot handle such interpretations, and these interpretations do not lead to breakthroughs of insight as one expects in psychotherapy with an adult. Although the girl and her parents usually come to understand some of the things that are transpiring between them, they usually do not profit from, nor can they tolerate, insight into unconscious motivations for their actions.

The role of the psychotherapist needs to be a flexible and a pragmatic one. The therapist must do whatever is appropriate to help the girl on her road to mastery, individuation, and separation. At times, the therapist will be the one who listens to her, as if she or he were (or, in fact, may be) her only friend. At other times, the therapist will be the limit setter who stops the girl when she cannot stop herself. Or, the therapist may be the adult she can turn to for help in understanding the world—the only adult she might talk to about her experimentation with sex or drugs or the only person she will allow to learn about her inadequacies. The therapist has to be a real person with whom the adolescent can identify and a reliable person whom she knows will be there when she needs help.

The psychotherapist will want to deal differently with the younger girl than with the older adolescent since the thought processes and the impulse control of these two age groups differ. The younger adolescent, under fifteen-and-a-half years old, is usually more impulsive, more action-oriented, less thoughtful, and less purposeful in her behavior than the older girl. The younger one is less separated from her parents and will usually accept their thoughts and statements without question or will oppose them in an equally unthinking manner. The younger girl frequently finds herself acting out without having planned it; she just acted. She is more impulse ridden, and her actions are more self-gratifying and without concern for future, or even present, consequences. With such an acting-out younger adolescent girl, the psychotherapist frequently will have to take control of the situation, limit the girl's behavior, and provide structure.

The younger girl who develops a clinical depression is often responding to one of her parent's appraisal of her, usually her mother's, as bad or worthless. Since she has separated very little from her parents, she is not in a good position to question her mother's estimation of her. With such a depressed younger adolescent, the therapist should take a strong stand against the girl's feelings of low self-worth. Sometimes the parents can be worked with and helped to see how their actions are affecting their daughter, but in certain situations the therapist should consider temporarily separating the girl from her parents.

Acting out in the older adolescent is usually more purposeful and less impulsive. The older girl knows what she is doing and her acting out is generally the result of a decision-making process, even though her reasoning may not seem logical to the adults in her life. Perhaps she is acting out because of despair, feeling that it does not make much difference *what* she does; she may be responding to the frustrations and failures she has experienced. Or, her acting out may be a plea for help with a family problem that she cannot resolve or sidestep. The therapist should help deter her acting out, but should also put a great deal of emphasis on discovering the problems and then helping her to handle them herself.

Because the older adolescent girl has a greater degree of separateness from her parents, her depression more closely resembles that of the adult than of the younger girl. The older adolescent is usually overwhelmed by some problem she faces. She may fear leaving her parents and respond with depression at one of the customary signposts of maturity, such as turning eighteen, graduating from high school, or starting college or a vocational training program. Sometimes the older adolescent cannot form an identity compatible with her own needs, skills, and aspirations and becomes depressed as she tries to do so. With such a depressed older adolescent, the psychotherapist should help her learn to cope with the demands of the world, make decisions, and act with self-confidence — or help her form a realistic and self-satisfying identity.

To successfully do psychotherapy with an adolescent girl, the therapist must be able to tolerate a great deal of dependency. The adolescent girl characteristically becomes very dependent on her therapist in one-on-one sessions. There are times, especially with the depressed adolescent, when the therapist should encourage the adolescent to become even more dependent for a while, in order to allow her to regress a bit and let herself be taken care of. Such a retreat will result in a temporary easing of the depression.

A therapist treating adolescent girls must watch for signs of countertransference within him- or herself. Working with young patients might revive a therapist's own adolescent struggles. It is easy for some therapists to condone the acting out of sexual urges or of angry and rebellious feelings toward authority figures in the adolescent patient—not because doing so is helpful for the patient but because they vicariously enjoy descriptions of the escapades or wish that they themselves could have acted out more in adolescence or young adulthood.

Finally, the adolescent girl must be allowed to separate from the therapist. Sometimes the adolescent girl will stop her psychotherapy suddenly, even before the therapist has seriously considered termination. The girl may need practice in separating from a significant person in her life. Separating from her therapist can afford her the opportunity to see how it feels; it may be a necessary part of her therapy. Learning to separate is, after all, one of the adolescent's developmental tasks. Even more important, the adolescent girl needs to feel that she can handle things on her own. She needs to feel that she can now make her own decisions. If she continues in her psychotherapy, she may feel that it is her therapist who is making the decisions, and she does not want to give her therapist credit for all her successes. She cannot do this and, at the same time, increase her self-confidence or develop a sense of mastery. She must come to learn that *she* can make decisions and can control her urges and impulses, and termination may be the ultimate sign that she can do so. Thus, an adolescent girl may leave her therapist suddenly or smugly, telling that person who has been so helpful, "I really don't understand psychotherapy, even after all this time." She may add, "You're a nice person, and I really respect you and all that, but I really don't see what you've done to help me. I'm better, that's for sure, but what have *you* done?" With no further ado, off she goes, feeling that she can handle the demands of the world. Hasn't she been doing so all along?

Selected
Annotated Bibliography

Aichorn, A. *Delinquency and Child Guidance*. New York: International Universities Press, 1964. (Originally pub. 1925.)

> Although the setting for this book is Austria over fifty
> years ago, a time when childrearing was culturally quite
> different from today, Aichorn's treatment of the delin-
> quent youths at Ober-Hollabrunn, a reform school, is a
> classic. His viewpoint is psychoanalytical and his princi-
> ples still apply today. He approaches the delinquent acts
> of the youth in a nonjudgmental and nonpunitive man-
> ner. Instead of punishing their misbehavior, he allows
> them to act out while he tries to fill some of their previ-
> ously unmet needs. He stresses the necessity for the boys to
> develop a strong, positive transference and gives examples
> of encouraging several of the youth to develop a strongly
> dependent transference on himself. These essays are very
> readable and his warmth, cunningness, and ingenuity
> show through in these scientific essays.

Blos, P. *On Adolescence*. New York: Free Press, 1962.

    This work is a classic in the field of the psychology of the adolescent. It is psychoanalytic in theory but obscurely written. Blos divides adolescence into early adolescence, adolescence proper, late adolescence, and postadolescence. In early adolescence the child starts separating from earlier object ties. Blos describes the decathexis of incestuous object ties and the free-floating libido, which clamors for new attachments. Because of the widening gap between the ego and the superego and the withdrawal of earlier object ties, the adolescent experiences a void or an impoverished feeling.

    Adolescence proper is characterized by the searching for new object relationships while simultaneously actively avoiding them. The female, more often than the male, finds a heterosexual object. Two predominant moods distinguish this period: *mourning,* following the renunciation of the parents, and *being in love,* the beginning of new object relationships. Late adolescence is a phase of consolidation. An idiosyncratic and stable arrangement of ego functions develops, a sense of autonomy grows, an irreversible sexual identity is selected, and an identity or self-concept is stabilized. He points to this period as the setting for the "identity crisis" described by Erikson. Postadolescence is the intervening phase between adolescence and adulthood, usually coinciding with occupational choice and the social roles of courtship, marriage, and adulthood. Blos uses the term *young adults* to describe the youth in this phase.

Blos, P. "The Second Individuation Process of Adolescence." In R. Eissler, A. Freud, H. Hartmann, and M. Kris (Eds.), *The Psychoanalytic Study of the Child.* Vol. 22. New York: International Universities Press, 1967.

    In this essay, Blos considers adolescence, not in its individual, developmental phases, but as a complete entity. He states that adolescence, in its totality, is a second individuation process, with the first process completed toward the end of the third year of life by attaining object constancy.

He reviews the first individuation process, described in 1963 by Mahler, when the child separates from the symbiotic bond with the mother and emerges as an individual toddler. Blos considers the adolescent's separation from the infantile object ties during adolescence a comparable, second individuation process, with the adolescent emerging as a separate adult in an adult world.

Blos describes the adolescent who acts out by running away, stealing a car, becoming promiscuous, or using drugs as "doing the wrong things for the right reasons." He considers these acts violent eruptions from the regressive pulls back to childhood and dependency and safety. Both this explanation for the adolescent's acting out and the concept of a second separation-individuation process in adolescence should be compared to Masterson (1972), who feels that such acting out in adolescence is a result of the fear of abandonment precipitated in the borderline adolescent who has not yet worked through his first individuation process.

Erikson, E. *Identity and the Life Cycle.* Psychological Issues Monograph 1. New York: International Universities Press, 1959.

Erikson describes the psychological tasks of the early phases of life and the crises the child must handle to grow into a healthy personality. During the first year of life the child must attain a sense of trust, which Erikson describes as an attitude toward oneself that is derived from first-year experiences. Without this trust, the person is likely to go through life with a basic stance of mistrust, pessimism, and an empty feeling.

From the age of one until almost age three, the child struggles between retention and letting go and should develop a sense of self-control without a loss of self-esteem. The task of this period is to develop a sense of autonomy without experiencing shame and doubt.

Between the ages of three and five, the child must acquire a sense of initiative without developing a sense of guilt. The mode of this phase is intrusive—the child intrudes into conversations, is aggressive, and is always on the lookout for rivals. Concurrently, the child develops a conscience, which could be punitive and primitive in demanding inhibition of all aggressiveness and initiative. During the school years, the child develops a sense of industry or a sense of inferiority, depending on school and life experiences.

Within this concept of specific developmental, psychological tasks of the various stages of childhood, Erikson states that at adolescence the child develops a sense of identity or suffers from identity diffusion.

Fraiberg, S. "Introduction to Therapy in Puberty." In R. Eissler, A. Freud, H. Hartmann, and E. Kris (Eds.), *The Psychoanalytic Study of the Child.* Vol. 10. New York: International Universities Press, 1955.

After surveying psychoanalytic literature on the relative difficulties of psychoanalysis at puberty, Fraiberg examines two cases of younger adolescent girls whom she treated with psychoanalysis, emphasizing their early reactions and some of the technical problems in starting treatment.

According to Fraiberg, many of the younger adolescent girls feel that they are going crazy if they are referred for psychoanalysis; this often increases the resistance to treatment, as does their fear of intimacy with a female analyst. If the younger adolescent girl fears that complete submission to the female psychoanalyst will be necessary, the initial resistance will increase.

Fraiberg writes about the dangers of interpretations in the psychoanalysis of a younger adolescent girl. She speaks of the adolescent's need for autonomy, which is stronger than her need for psychoanalysis or for relief of symptoms, and warns of the relative weakness of the adolescent's ego; the symptom formed by the adolescent may protect the ego from being overwhelmed by affect. Fraiberg does not make an interpretation to an adolescent girl until she has determined that the adolescent can handle lesser amounts of the affect involved; she does not wish to weaken a necessary defense. Fraiberg reminds us that the ego needs to maintain control over drives, a sometimes tenuous control during adolescence; she hesitates therefore to make any interpretations that undermine the ego's control.

This essay offers a great deal of thoughtful advice to all therapists who work with adolescent girls.

Gittleson, M. "Character Synthesis: The Psychotherapeutic Problem of Adolescence." *American Journal of Orthopsychiatry*, 1948, *18*, 422–431.

In this article, Gittleson makes several points that are crucial to understanding and treating the psychopathology of the adolescent patient. Some psychotherapists avoid working with the adolescent patient because, unlike working with the adult or with the child patient, the psychotherapist may have difficulty maintaining the controlled emotional increment between himself and the patient. The adolescent patient puts the therapist's integrity to its severest test.

Gittleson compares the limited transference capabilities of the adolescent patient to similar limitations in the narcissistic and the borderline patient. When the adolescent patient tells the therapist what he feels the therapist is like, the patient is expressing his current, true opinion. The patient is not displacing onto the therapist impressions of significant persons in his past. The therapist who works with adolescents must be capable of tolerating this.

The therapist and the therapeutic relationship must provide the patient with a proper balance between dependable security and developmental stimulation, and a balance between control and ego ideal. He stresses that the therapist must provide a dependable relationship for the adolescent patient because of his vulnerability and adds that this dependability of the relationship is more important than the *dependency* so many have written about.

In this classic writing, Gittleson quotes other writers extensively and includes a comprehensive bibliography.

Grinker, R. "Mentally Healthy Young Males (Homoclites)." *Archives of General Psychiatry,* 1962, *6,* 405–453.

This article describes a significant study done on "normal" male freshmen at George Williams College. The young men were questioned about their adolescent experiences and their relationship with their parents during their adolescence. Grinker identified thirty-one young men whom he called "the very well-adjusted group" and thirty-one young men who he called "the marginally adjusted group." The determination of the success of their adjustment was made on a stability-liability axis.

In the very well-adjusted group, few showed any evidence of impulsivity during their adolescence. In the marginally adjusted group, only four young men told of prior rebelliousness and antisocial activity, involving theft or court probation for disorderly conduct. All four, interestingly enough, spontaneously told of persistent childhood enuresis, which Grinker saw "as a remarkable confirmation of Michaels (1955) theory that persistent enuresis is a psychosomatic manifestation of the lack of internal inhibition just as delinquency reflects a later sociopsychological defect in inhibition" (p. 449).

Grinker described three common coping mechanisms used by these subjects: physical activity, denial, and isolation. Surprised that he found so little adolescent rebelliousness, Grinker called this group of young men *homoclites,* ordinary persons who follow the common rule.

Group for the Advancement of Psychiatry. *Normal Adolescence: Its Dynamics and Impacts.* New York: Scribner's, 1968.

This is a typical Group for the Advancement of Psychiatry (GAP) report where the contributions of knowledgeable and distinguished persons in their fields are written, reviewed, and re-reviewed by the whole committee so many times that anything controversial, thought provoking or even original is completely washed out before the printing. Nonetheless, this GAP report is well written and presents a brief review of the currently accepted ideas in the field of normal adolescence and is therefore an important reference and starting point for the study of psychotherapy with adolescents.

Holmes, D. *The Adolescent in Psychotherapy.* Boston: Little, Brown, 1964.

Holmes' very readable book describes techniques of dealing with various aspects of psychotherapy with adolescents. He discusses several aspects of adolescents' personalities that are potential assets for psychotherapy. Adolescents, Holmes feels, are strongly motivated to move ahead in life and, if necessary, will use psychotherapy to help accomplish this. Adolescents are deeply curious about adults and their lives; this curiosity can be helpful in psychotherapy. Also, adolescents have an awareness of the future, which younger children lack, making adolescents more motivated to change or to consider alternatives for their future.

Holmes professes to have an eclectic viewpoint, feeling that in psychotherapy, one does what works and the philosophy comes later. He describes a very active role for psychotherapists — active in talking about themselves, active in giving advice, and active in setting limits on inappropriate behavior. Most of the discussion in this book centers around inpatient psychotherapy, but outpatient psychotherapy is discussed as well.

In his preface, Holmes promises to use a minimal amount of technical language, which he accomplishes, and creates a book that is not only interesting to read but also gives the reader the feeling of what psychotherapy is like with an adolescent.

Johnson, A. "Sanctions for Superego Lacunae." In K. Eissler (Ed.), *Searchlights on Delinquency.* New York: International Universities Press, 1949.

In this classic essay on dealing with delinquent children, Johnson coins the term *superego lacunae* to describe the deficiencies in their superegos. These children identified with parents who had similar lacks in their superegos — they were similarly delinquent.

In the treatment of such children, Johnson proposes that it is of little value to belittle the child's parents or to point out to the child their shortcomings — the child is already aware of them. She warns that therapists working with such children must keep their promises and never make unrealistic promises just to ease immediate pain. Therapists should note little inconsistencies and dishonesty of the child at the outset, even before a transference develops, and set limits or guidelines for the patient to clearly show what behavior is permissible. According to Johnson, these steps aid the child more than helping him understand why he behaves as he does.

Josselyn, I. "The Ego in Adolescence." *American Journal of Orthopsychiatry*, 1954, *24*, 223-237.

In classical psychoanalytic terminology, Josselyn very thoughtfully describes the role of and the pressures on the ego during adolescence. She defines a *strong ego* as one that is capable of finding a resolution to the many pressures it is exposed to, while a *weak ego* is not capable of making such integrations.

In adolescence, the ego needs to adjust to a biologically different self. Identification with parents, a source of support to children, is not similarly supportive to adolescents. To be like the parent is no longer a source of self-respect but rather a cause for self-depreciation. As they enter adolescence, children still have archaic superegos. Rules that were valid in childhood are no longer valid in adolescence; the superego, too, must change. In addition to all these strains, Josselyn recalls that Erikson pointed out that our society does not have clear-cut roles and behavior standards for the adolescent. Society does not offer the adolescent much support. These pressures can result in "ego exhaustion," which Josselyn feels is the characteristic syndrome of adolescence.

Lorand, S. "Adolescent Depression." *International Journal of Psychoanalysis*, 1967, *48*, 53-59.

In this article, Lorand discusses the similarity of depression in adults and depression in adolescents — both depressions result from a loss. The loss adolescents experience results from detachment from parental ties. They feel abandoned by those previously relied on for support and guidance.

After commenting on Bibrings's view of depression as partial loss of self-esteem and Freud's definition of the ego ideal and its relation to the superego, Lorand introduces the concept of psychotherapists acting as transient ego ideals because of patients' identification with their psychotherapists. By serving as transient ego ideals, psychotherapists can help patients acquire the capabilities of understanding, permissiveness, and love.

Lorand feels that the acting out of adolescents serves a purpose for patients. He considers cheating, lying, and gambling a defense against feeling inferior. The self-destructive acting out of adolescents is a reaction to stress, but the aim of the acting out is to force the environment to provide them with love and caring.

Masterson, J. *The Psychiatric Dilemma of Adolescence.* Boston: Little, Brown, 1967.

This book presents a study of 101 adolescent outpatients, who sought psychotherapy, and a study of 101 adolescents in a comparison group, who came from twenty-six of the sixty-six high schools represented in the patient sample. Masterson describes the diagnoses and gives case examples of the patient group and shows that adolescents do not tend to outgrow their symptoms with time.

The comparison between the patient group and the control group is most interesting. In both groups, the adolescents complained of depression and anxiety in roughly comparable numbers, but the degree and intensity of these symptoms in the patient group were considerably greater than in the comparison group. In the other areas that Masterson considered — acting out, immaturity, schizophrenia, sexual difficulties, hypochondriacal tendencies, hysterical symptoms, and conversion symptoms — the patient group showed more adolescents with these problems than did the comparison group. The symptoms in the control group were much less intense and caused much less impairment than did the symptoms in the patient group. Masterson concludes that, "Although we must continue to view adolescent turmoil as a universal psychodynamic factor, its clinical effects are surely less significant than previously thought." Readers should note Chapters Two and Thirteen, which describe the methodology and selection of the groups and the results. The other chapters deal mainly with problems of diagnosis.

Masterson, J. *Treatment of the Borderline Adolescent*. New York: Wiley, 1972.

This discussion of the psychopathology and treatment of the adolescent with a borderline personality assumes that the borderline adolescent has not yet worked through the separation-individuation process that should have occurred by the third year of life, when the infant breaks the symbiotic bond with the mother and becomes an individual. Separation from the family, which is occurring in adolescence, re-creates the intense anxiety and fear of death or abandonment these borderline individuals experienced earlier at the time of separation-individuation. Masterson feels that the mothers of these borderline adolescents suffer from a borderline state themselves. In adolescents, according to Masterson, the signs of this syndrome are not easily recognized; the adolescents will act out by failing to achieve or abusing street drugs.

Masterson feels that a two-phase treatment program—a fairly prolonged inpatient stay followed by outpatient treatment—is necessary for these adolescents. The treatment and the dynamics presented in this book are well described and are very thought provoking. This work insists on a long, initial inpatient stay without adequate documentation of its necessity.

Meeks, J. *The Fragile Alliance*. Baltimore: Williams and Wilkins, 1971.

This book deals mainly with outpatient psychotherapy

with the adolescent patient. Meeks begins by discussing the pressures that adolescents face, their way of thinking, and some of the meanings of their behavior. He examines the psychotherapist's qualifications necessary for good psychotherapy with the adolescent patient. He stresses the need for the psychotherapist to be an adult and to behave like one, to be pragmatic and tactful.

An especially valuable part of this book is Meeks' analysis and description of establishing a therapeutic alliance with the adolescent patient. He reminds the reader that psychotherapy is classically an alliance between the psychotherapist and the observing part of the patient's ego. In the adolescent, one may find little observing part of the ego. Meeks notes, however, that the adolescent typically finds some special friend who possesses some of the personality characteristics that the adolescent feels she or he lacks. The adolescent then tends to idealize this friend and finally identifies with this special friend and incorporates the desired personality traits. The psychotherapist who deals with the adolescent patient can try to become such a special friend to the adolescent patient and, in this manner, establish a fragile therapeutic alliance. Because the alliance is fragile he suggests that the psychotherapist should avoid approving or disapproving of the adolescent patient's behavior for fear of being compared to the patient's superego.

Miller, A. "Identification and Adolescent Development." In S. Feinstein and P. Giovacchini (Eds.), *Adolescent Psychiatry*. Vol. 2. New York: Basic Books, 1973.

Miller discusses the psychic restructuring that occurs during adolescence, particularly from the viewpoint of the identification process, in which adolescents identify with models, roles, and transactions that are available throughout their adolescence.

Miller makes an especially interesting point when discussing the changes occurring in how adolescents view themselves and in how they view their parents. As their self-representation changes, their object representations must also change, especially those of their parents. There seems to be some reciprocity in this process. So that their own ego can become less vulnerable and more powerful, adolescents must come to view their parents in a more realistic light and therefore adolescence is characterized by some disillusionment with the parents' strength.

Miller, M., and Roberts, L. "Psychotherapy with the Children of Charismatic Individuals." *American Journal of Psychiatry,* 1967, *123,* 1049-1057.

This article presents the idea that the child of a charismatic individual may have greater difficulty achieving an individual identity and may have less opportunity for self-realization than a child of a less charismatic person.

The authors review *Cradles of Eminence* by Goertzel and Goertzel, which indicates that of the 400 famous persons studied about one half had fathers who were failure prone, especially financially. Only twenty-one of the 400 eminent persons had fathers who were described as powerful, dominating individuals.

When the children of famous and charismatic individuals enter psychotherapy, it is easy for the psychotherapist to enjoy descriptions of the parent; the child is familiar with this interest in the parent. The authors feel that it can be a corrective emotional experience for the patient if the psychotherapy centers around subjects other than the parent. The psychotherapist dealing with such patients should not attempt to destroy the image of the charismatic parent in the eyes of the patient or to take the parent's place.

Monson, R., and Gorman, B. "Sibling Set Composition and Female Occupational Achievement." *Sociological Symposium: Sociology of Women, Part I,* 1976, *15,* 69-75.

Monson and Gorman studied 485 achieving females, especially in respect to their birth order in their family. The criteria for achievement included a doctorate degree, current affiliation with a university that granted graduate degrees, the rank of assistant professor or better, and employment in the fields of biology, chemistry, psychology, or sociology. In addition, the women were all born in the United States.

This article refers to studies indicating that in men there is a strong correlation between occupational achievement and position in the sibling set composition. Only sons, the eldest son in a small family, or the youngest son in a large family are the most likely to be occupational achievers.

In Monson and Gorman's study, the women most often came from small, urban families, with a high proportion of Jewish families and a low proportion of Catholic families. Unlikely to be only children, these women were most often the eldest children and generally did not have brothers.

Offer, D. *The Psychological World of the Teenager*. New York: Basic Books, 1969.

Offer studied seventy-three boys for four years, starting with their freshman year in high school. The study included periodic interviews with the boys, interviews with their parents, school reports, and occasional psychological testing. Boys with obviously severe psychopathology were eliminated from the study, as were boys who were obviously exceptionally well adjusted. Offer wanted a group of model boys; they came from two suburban high schools.

Offer found that relatively few of these boys showed difficulty controlling their impulses during their adolescence, and they showed no strikingly deviant behavior. He describes several different coping mechanisms the boys used, such as physical activity to sublimate their drives, facing their problems rather than trying to avoid them, and relying on humor extensively. They found great satisfaction in their achievements and accomplishments.

Twenty-five percent of the boys in the study participated in some sort of delinquent act during their adolescence, including stealing, throwing bottles on the highway, vandalism — sometimes just a matter of overthrowing a garbage can after an exciting game — and fighting: that was sometimes serious. Offer concluded that delinquency was only one route through adolescence and that his subjects did not choose that route.

Offer, D., and Offer, J. "Normal Adolescence in Perspective." In J. Schoolar (Ed.), *Current Issues in Adolescent Psychotherapy.* New York: Brunner/Mazel, 1973.

Offer and Offer did a carefully planned factor analysis of fifty-five different sociopsychological factors in this same group of seventy-three boys studied and reported on in 1969. By observing the clustering that was found through factor analysis, the authors determined that adolescent boys take one of three different paths through adolescence, which they call *the continuous growth group, the surgent growth group,* and *the tumultuous growth group.*

In the continuous growth group, the adolescent boys had no apparent tensions between themselves and their parents. There was also no evidence of acting out or impulsivity. Their parents seemed to enjoy the boys' increasing maturity and adjusted to it well. In the surgent growth group, there was some discord between the boys and their parents. These boys appeared to be more action oriented, remained close to their parents, and handled well the expected stresses of life; with unexpected stress, they tended to use projection and anger. In the tumultuous growth group, the youths had a stormy adolescence. These boys frequently came from lower socioeconomic backgrounds and there was occasionally a history of mental illness in their families. One third of this group ended up in some sort of counseling or psychotherapy.

Parker, B. *My Language is Me.* New York: Basic Books, 1962.

Parker's book is a detailed descriptive account of her psychotherapy with a disturbed, probably preschizophrenic, sixteen-year-old boy who had much difficulty communicating with people; in the beginning, he can hardly communicate with his therapist. He thinks of himself only in mechanistic terms and talks about such things as cars, sparks, and power. Psychotherapy helps him and his therapist better understand this symbolic language. This case report has many long, verbatim excerpts of the psycho-therapy, interspersed with discussion of the treatment techniques. The book reads like a novel but teaches a great deal to people who wish to work with disturbed adolescents.

References

Aichorn, A. *Delinquency and Child Guidance.* New York: International Universities Press, 1964. (Originally pub. 1925.)

Blos, P. *On Adolescence.* New York: Free Press, 1962.

Blos, P. "The Second Individuation Process of Adolescence." In R. Eissler, A. Freud, H. Hartman, and M. Kris (Eds.), *The Psychoanalytic Study of the Child.* Vol. 22. New York: International Universities Press, 1967.

Bourne, P., and Ramsen, A. "The Therapeutic Community Phenomenon." *Journal of Psychedelic Drugs,* 1975, *7,* 203-207.

Erikson, E. *Identity and the Life Cycle.* Psychological Issues Monograph 1. New York: International Universities Press, 1959.

Fraiberg, S. "Introduction to Therapy in Puberty." In R. Eissler, A. Freud, H. Hartman, and E. Kris (Eds.), *The Psychoanalytic Study of the Child.* Vol. 10. New York: International Universities Press, 1955.

Giovacchini, P., "The Adolescent Process and Character Formation." In S. Feinstein and P. Giovacchini (Eds.), *Adolescent Psychiatry.* Vol. 2. New York: Basic Books, 1973.

Gittleson, M. "Character Synthesis: The Psychotherapeutic Problem of Adolescence." *American Journal of Orthopsychiatry,* 1948, *18,* 422–431.

Goertzel, V., and Goertzel, M. *Cradles of Eminence.* Boston: Little, Brown, 1962.

Grinker, R. "Mentally Healthy Young Males (Homoclites)." *Archives of General Psychiatry,* 1962, *6,* 405–453.

Group for the Advancement of Psychiatry. *Normal Adolescence: Its Dynamics and Impact.* New York: Scribner's, 1968.

Henderson, S., and others. "An Assessment of Hostility in a Population of Adolescents." *Archives of General Psychiatry,* 1977, *34,* 706–711.

Hogarty, G., and others. "Drug and Sociotherapy in the Aftercare of Schizophrenic Patients." *Archives of General Psychiatry,* 1974, *31,* 609–618.

Holmes, D. *The Adolescent in Psychotherapy.* Boston: Little, Brown, 1964.

Howells, J. (Ed.). *Modern Perspectives in Adolescent Psychiatry.* New York: Brunner/Mazel, 1971.

Hudgens, R. *Psychiatric Disorders in Adolescence.* Baltimore: Williams and Wilkins, 1974.

Johnson, A. "Sanctions for Superego Lacunae." In K. Eissler (Ed.), *Searchlights On Delinquency.* New York: International Universities Press, 1949.

Josselyn, I. "The Ego in Adolescence." *American Journal of Orthopsychiatry,* 1954, *24,* 223–237.

King, S. "Coping Mechanisms in Adolescents." *Psychiatric Annals,* 1971, *3,* 10–46.

Lamb, D., Fernelius, K., and Switzer, C. "A Therapeutic Detention Program for Adolescents on Court Probation." *Hospital and Community Psychiatry,* 1973, *24,* 618–620.

Lamb, H. R. "Individual Psychotherapy: Helping the Long-Term Patient Achieve Mastery." In H. R. Lamb and Associates, *Community Survival for Long-Term Patients.* San Francisco: Jossey-Bass, 1976.

Lindemann, E. "Symptomatology and Management of Acute Grief." *American Journal of Psychiatry,* 1944, *101,* 141–148.

Lorand, S. "Adolescent Depression." *International Journal of Psychoanalysis,* 1967, *48,* 53–59.

Masterson, J. *The Psychiatric Dilemma of Adolescence.* Boston: Little, Brown, 1967.

Masterson, J. *Treatment of the Borderline Adolescent.* New York: Wiley, 1972.

Masterson, J. "The Borderline Adolescent." In S. Feinstein and P. Giovacchini (Eds.), *Adolescent Psychiatry.* Vol. 2. New York: Basic Books, 1973.

Meeks, J. *The Fragile Alliance.* Baltimore: Williams and Wilkins, 1971.

Miller, A. "Identification and Adolescent Development." In S. Feinstein and P. Giovacchini (Eds.), *Adolescent Psychiatry.* Vol. 2. New York: Basic Books, 1973.

Miller, D. *Adolescence, Psychology, Psychopathology, and Psychotherapy.* New York: Aronson, 1974.

Miller, M., and Roberts, L. "Psychotherapy with the Children of Charismatic Individuals." *American Journal of Psychiatry,* 1967, *123*, 1049–1057.

Monson, R., and Gorman, B. "Sibling Set Composition and Female Occupational Achievement." *Sociological Symposium: Sociology of Women, Part I,* 1976, *15*, 69–75.

Offer, D. *The Psychological World of the Teenager.* New York: Basic Books, 1969.

Offer D., and Offer, J. "Profiles of Normal Adolescent Girls." *Archives of General Psychiatry,* 1968, *19*, 513–522.

Offer, D., and Offer, J. "Normal Adolescence in Perspective." In J. Schoolar (Ed.), *Current Issues in Adolescent Psychotherapy.* New York: Brunner/Mazel, 1973.

Piaget, J. "Intellectual Development of the Adolescent." In A. Esman (Ed.), *The Psychology of Adolescence.* New York: International Universities Press, 1975.

Spiegel, L. "A Review of Contributions to a Theory of Adolescence." In R. Eissler, A. Freud, H. Hartman, and E. Kris (Eds.), *The Psychoanalytic Study of the Child.* Vol. 6. New York: International Universities Press, 1951.

Teicher, J. "A Solution to the Chronic Problem of Living: Adolescent Attempted Suicide." In J. Schoolar (Ed.), *Current Issues in Adolescent Psychiatry.* New York: Brunner/Mazel, 1973.

Yablonsky, L. *Synanon: The Tunnel Back.* New York: Penguin Books, 1965.

Index